Obstacles Equal Opportunities In Business

Volume III

Compiled by Heather Andrews

http://www.getyouvisible.com/

Print ISBN: 978-1-989848-27-2
E-book ISBN: 978-1-989848-28-9

Table of Contents

Gratitude

I want to thank the co-authors that contributed to this book for their vulnerability and willingness to share their knowledge. Their stories are powerful, and their wisdom will offer you the path to changing your business story.

I am grateful to my fantastic publishing team:

My editor, Suzanne LaVoie, helps guide and coach our authors through the process of sharing their stories despite their fears. My graphic designer, Robin Albright, spent countless hours and revisions to get the cover and Vision just right.

I am grateful to you, our readers. Thank you for being a part of our journey.

I am grateful for the lessons I have learned through all my obstacles that helped bring the opportunities that I have encountered.
I am glad we are finally bringing these stories to the world so we can openly discuss, learn, and grow together for a stronger future for ourselves and to serve our community.

Hugs,
Heather

Foreword

When Heather asked me to write the foreword for this book, I was super excited because I have overcome a lifetime of obstacles to growing a Women's empowerment empire, Womanition, with expansion into Vavasaur, a leadership platform for men this year. These platforms enhance and expand my business realm to help men and women to achieve success. I call my success "irrational optimism," meaning absolute faith in myself and my objectives in the face of all adversity.

Heather came into my world five years ago as a new entrepreneur, so she knows firsthand what Womanition can create when our system is implemented. As a proud publisher, I have entirely transformed Womanition Magazine into a multiple award-winning annual publication showcasing women in business while promoting their products and services. Vavasaur for men is next. Knowing myself now, one would find it difficult to believe that, as a little girl, I used to cower in the closet, holding my hand over my younger sister's mouth to ensure silence. It was best to hide at certain times, so her drunken, abusive father wouldn't be able to beat them for some imagined offense.

My father is long gone, but I marvel about my mother's fortitude in the face of his frequent tantrums. "*I cannot believe how she put up with so much with the beatings and insults. I now understand she felt she didn't deserve to be treated with respect because of what she lived and learned from her parents. It's tough for kids to grow up to be responsible adults when your role models are so dysfunctional."*

Yet, growing up responsibly, I was able to move past it. My passion project, Womanition, has radically improved countless entrepreneurs' lives and launched many a successful business. Womanition is now a much admired, multi-faceted phenomenon committed to uniting, educating, supporting, and promoting business power. Much more than just the magazine, this thriving venture encompasses everything from a highly sought-after mentoring program to entrepreneur networking meetings in five different locations. Along with awards opportunities and business events, there is also a flourishing non-profit, ACES - A Community Engaged in Sharing and Vavasaur-Leader of Men Magazine and Community. With Heather Andrews purchasing the Southern Alberta License for Womanition and expanding into new communities for men and women, 2022 into 2023 will bring about more ways to serve our communities.

As a business owner, I want to share the pillars I have lived by to grow and overcome adversity.

INTEGRITY - the quality of being honest and having strong moral principles.

Integrity is, undoubtedly, one of the most important qualities to possess in life!

I refuse to do business with anyone who doesn't follow through on what they say they intend to do, when, and how they promise to do it. If you commit, you have an obligation to live up to it unless there are extenuating circumstances. Otherwise, how can someone possibly trust what you say?

I will never forget the experience of being hired by one of my friends to publish a series of monthly magazines featuring various builders in the interior of B.C. Each issue was supported by that particular builder's sub-trades, presumably buying advertising. What an eye-opener! I was on the third builders' magazine, with 125 trades involved. I considered this an enormous amount considering that the typical number of trades was between 60 and 65.

Here I was, congratulating myself on such a potentially huge magazine. Little did I know, this fellow wasn't paying his sub-trades on time, so, needless to say, they were not overly eager to support him. When I called on his behalf, I was met by a torrent of profanity, bitterness, and rejection that would reduce me to tears every day. It was just devastating!

I was this close to quitting and moving back home with my tail between my legs when my niece sent me the famous Napoleon Hill book, **Think and Grow Rich.** I read that book every day, and Hill's words inspired me. Never give up! I only had three weeks to the deadline on this builders' magazine despite all this negativity and refusal. I only had three weeks to send in my advertisements, photos, and copy to get this magazine published on time, and Hill's book helped me move through the panic. When I sent it to the printer, it was just over the guaranteed dollar amount! I DID IT!

What a proud moment for me!

Even though this happened about thirty years ago, I remember it like it was yesterday. My friend asked me later on why I didn't just quit. I remember I said, "I gave you my word, so I had to finish it." Doing something right is always memorable because you feel good inside. If you don't have integrity, you have nothing I want.

RESPONSIBILITY – the opportunity or ability to act independently and make decisions without authorization.

A great leader must take full responsibility for every aspect of their business, especially when there's a problem. Any issues should be resolved immediately, not ignored. Even if a staff member is the one who made a mistake, the responsibility lies with the boss, the person in charge. I will always take the heat for their errors. So, you always need to be careful who you ask to represent your company. Instead of setting you up for success, the wrong person could drag you down and ruin your brand.

I have been publishing magazines for more than thirty years. I can tell you, no matter how thoroughly the material gets proofed, there will inevitably be a mistake. Maybe it's a period that gets dropped or something tiny like that, but an error nonetheless. My people are only human, and humans are not perfect. I do my very best to make it up to the buyer, to compensate them effectively so that they'll continue to give me their business.

I pride myself on being a problem solver. There is always a solution, even if it's just to do nothing. Always consider how your decision will affect others and choose the course of action least detrimental to everyone involved. Doing the right thing is not always the easy thing.

COMMITMENT - a pledge or undertaking - the state or quality of being dedicated to a cause, activity, etc.

Once I commit to someone or something, I involve myself completely. I give it my all! When I was younger, searching for my ultimate career, I spent five years dedicated to the real estate business. I was driven! At the time, it was everything.

I always worked extremely hard to be the top salesperson in the company, accomplishing this regularly. Along with selling houses, I even took on the main management position. When the company went under, I blamed myself. Knowing my feelings of failure, the operations manager of the real estate firm put things in perspective for me. He explained that even if I brought in a hundred thousand dollars a month in revenue, it would not have been enough to save the company. This downfall had nothing to do with me at all. What a relief! However, I had lost my passion for home sales and never could feel quite as motivated again. My real estate career was over.

People will eventually see right through you if your only motivator is money. When you know your WHY, your overall reason for doing what you do, the rest seems to fall into place.

HONESTY - moral correctness, uprightness, fairness

If you're having a horrible day and someone asks how you're doing, chances are you'll say you're wonderful even though you're not. Technically, that is a lie, but let's face it, it's not professional for you, as a leader, to go around telling everyone you're having a lousy day. It's not their business, and it's not good for your business.

When you tell a blatant lie about your product or service, however, that is unacceptable as it leads people to buy under false pretenses. Calling yourself an expert or a professional is also dishonest when you don't have the experience or credentials to back up your claims. When you lie, it comes back to haunt you. Always tell the truth, and you'll never have to worry about what you told who.

AMBITION - a strong desire to do or to achieve something, typically requiring determination and hard work

Despite my challenging upbringing, I always knew I was different from the rest of my siblings. I had ambition! From a young age, I was always in a leadership role in the games we'd play. I knew even then that I wanted to be my own boss.

Well, here I am, proof positive that we do create our reality. I am so grateful for being able to set my own hours and work from home. I love that I have the power to always do what I think is right and correct in my business. So far, I have achieved success like I never thought I would or believed I could!

When I put my mind to something, I usually make it happen. Now, whether it's successful or not is another thing. Years back, I took a risk and started a pet section in my health and wellness publication. Big mistake! I might have thought it was a brilliant idea, but I should have done the research to see if anyone else agreed!

ACCEPTANCE - the action of consenting to receive or undertake something offered

I have accepted that, out of all the people on this earth, only 20% make the real effort while the other 80% sit back and complain. Everywhere you look, you see certain people making it, becoming a success in their business and in life, while others look on wondering why they're not doing as well. They can even be highly envious! I accepted a long time ago that nothing would happen in my life unless I made it happen. All I had to do was get to work.

As a teenager, I desperately wanted a $28 pair of shoes. My single mother had six kids to feed and clothe, so there was no way I was getting that money from her, and rightly so. I accepted that as well. So I went to work myself and, very soon, I had those shoes. Great lesson!

So now, when I want something badly enough, I know I have to get to work and make it happen. I believe I can have anything I want.

PATIENCE - the capacity to accept or tolerate delay, trouble, or suffering without getting angry or upset.

Mastering patience is a challenge for me. I am slow to anger, but I have been known to explode when I do. Having a friend or confidante you trust is very helpful in diffusing your upset during challenging times. I have a few friends with whom I can spout off, let my guard down and be myself without fear of repercussions.

Some business people just don't understand how to take responsibility for their actions. Also, some people are not gracious and harp on silly little things that can be rectified almost immediately. If you calm down and think clearly, you'll realize how unimportant they are. Don't sweat the small stuff!

Sometimes the right thing to do in your business is to ensure that one or two "bad apples" are not poisoning the whole group. When it's evident from their feedback that a large number of people are unhappy about someone else's behavior, it's time for that person to be asked to leave. You have to take the right action for your business.

OPTIMISM - hopefulness and confidence about the future or the successful outcome of something

Competition excites me. I love to win, but money has never been a major motivator for me. A strong, inspiring belief in a person or a cause is ultimately more conducive to my success.

Winning all the way is my motto, winning despite all odds. Never would I do something and even consider for a minute that it would not succeed. I call it irrational optimism. On the other hand, if now is not the time for me to win, I don't get all bent out of shape and refuse to let go. I simply say "next" and move on.

FORGIVENESS - a conscious, deliberate decision to release feelings of resentment or vengeance toward a person or group who has harmed you, regardless of whether they actually deserve your forgiveness.

When you forgive someone, you rid yourself of your negative feelings surrounding an incident for which they were responsible. It doesn't ever mean, however, that you excuse or condone their bad behavior. I can release people from my life instantly. Once someone has hurt someone I love or has done something to me that's, to my mind, unforgivable, they are gone. It's like we were never close at all.

Holding on means trying to push life into a place of your own making despite it not being a good fit or having the right timing. Letting go means being willing to allow life to carry you to a new place.

HAPPINESS - a sense of well-being, joy, or contentment. When people are successful, safe, or lucky, they feel happiness.

I remember, many years ago, taking a course where the question was asked, "Are you happy 51% or more of the time?" My answer is still, "Yes!" I have never been happier than I am today. Some say happiness is wanting what you have. If that's true, then I must be ecstatic. I cannot think of anything that I absolutely have to have. I'm content.

LIFE'S LESSONS

In some ways, I had a very challenging upbringing, but because of this, I have learned many valuable lessons. Some realizations came to me easily, whereas others have taken me years to understand. All in all, it was for the greater good. I really like the person I've become.

At one time, I used to think I was a coward, but then, in the act of standing up for myself, I realized I was actually very courageous. I also thought I was lazy. Eventually, I figured out it was really fear that was keeping me in place. Now, I know that despite being afraid of what might happen, I have to step forward and take the risk.

My two unhappy marriages came about because of me settling for the unacceptable. I thought I was unworthy, and I deserved less. Now, I boldly ask for what I want and avoid what I don't.

It's difficult to believe that what I admired as "cool" is so disgusting to me now.

I've discovered that, in reality, I am actually quite introverted. Even though, as the leader of Womanition, I do need to be more extroverted and socialize with peers, what truly charges my energy is being alone at home. I can't see retirement as a positive choice for me at this time. I want to keep growing Womanition. I simply love the community, this family of women I've created, and each and every member within.

Yes, I am satisfied with all I have accomplished. I take pride in the fact that I did the hard work to make it all happen! That's what it takes. You have to do the work. Now, I reap the rewards and look forward to making a positive difference in the lives of many more women. As the old eighties song says, "My future's so bright, I gotta wear shades."

MY TAKE-A-WAYS

1. Don't take advantage of others.

If you want people to pay you, then you need to pay them. Everyone should be able to pay a fair price.

2. You reap what you sow.
   If you lie to people, they will lie to you. If you cheat others, others will cheat on you.

3. Do what you say you're going to do, even if it almost kills you.

I hope you find these lessons and this book inspiring and helpful so you can go and create your award-winning life and business.

Dorothy Briggs

Publisher/Founder

Dorothy@womanition.com

womanition.com

Introduction

Obstacles. Challenges. Trials. World Pandemic.

This book came about as the last two years wreaked havoc on my business. Yet as I watched, connected, and learned from others, I knew success could still be ours.

I observed people pivoting to online platforms; this shifted how we learn, connect, and navigate technology as there was no option. In this new world, new business opportunities were created. Cryptocurrency grew. As people were locked down and lost jobs, the #1 google search became how to make money online? Networking marketing companies exploded as a result. People were carrying out technology platform webinars. The power of the pause allowed people to reflect on how they wanted to live their lives, and many chose not to return to work as they were achieving success and generating revenue in other ways.

Entrepreneurship is a skill; it requires tenacity for those days when it is difficult. Your desire to create and operate your business needs to be anchored into your why and how you serve your clients. The team you build to support you in your business is critical as these people are dealing with your clients, your money, and your brand.

This book was derived from the onset of new entrepreneurs that I observed start businesses in the last few years. My desire and the co-authors in this book were to provide you, the entrepreneur, with inspiration, tools, strategies, and how to operate your businesses for the upward trajectory and long term.

I'm thrilled you've chosen to join 11 of my inspiring co-authors and me as we delve into the topic of overcoming the odds to create successful businesses, relationships, and lives.

Throughout this book, we aim to ignite your confidence and drive to overcome whatever challenge you happen to be up against with authenticity, vulnerability, and good old-fashioned grit. We also hope to help you expose the humbling wisdom in the lesson and learn how to change your circumstances by shifting your mindset—*choosing* to win from now on.

You'll also discover how our brave authors learned how to thrive in the face of adversity as they tackled the obstacles set in front of them and systematically overcame what was holding them back. These powerful personal stories are a testament to the human spirit and how resilient we can be when we set our minds to it.

Collectively, we hope you can gain insight into how to overcome adversity in your own life by sharing our experiences, our lessons learned, and the mindset tips from each co-author. From a personal standpoint, this book is yet another milestone in my professional evolution, which would not have been possible without the challenges I had thrown at me in the last six years. Every obstacle has been a blessing in disguise.

Win or learn; we need to keep moving *forward.*

Heather

Carrie Tuttle

Carrie supports professionals to inject more energy and meaning into their work. As a seasoned sales and marketing executive and certified coach, she works with leaders to identify and improve the mindset and skillset barriers that hold them back. Then, establish healthy, productive habits that help them perform at their best.

In her professional career, she has led teams locally and virtually at the Director level. She has coached and consulted with Fortune 500 companies across North America.

Carrie has a Bachelor of Commerce degree from The University of Calgary. Her interest in human emotions and motivation lead her to study and be formally trained from Coaches Training Institute (CTI).

As a coach, Carrie is both pragmatic and empathetic. She helped an award-winning leader redefine himself while selling his company and a consultant to double her rates within four months and another to reposition herself in more meaningful work.

Connect with Carrie:

https://www.teammojo.ca/

https://www.linkedin.com/in/1carrietuttle/

https://www.instagram.com/carrieatuttle

Chapter 1

From Widow to Wonder Woman

By Carrie Tuttle

Only five years ago, I was a new widow with a 2-year-old son, stuck in an unfulfilling, golden-handcuffs job, and had no idea how I was going to make it all work. Today, I'm looking at the sun streaming in through the window of my home office, loving my work, and looking forward to every day I get to live my life.

It hasn't been an easy journey, and my story is still being written. In retrospect, I've come a long way in a short time. Here's how it happened and what I learned along the way.

I had a very predictable, well-paying job in financial services with an impressive portfolio of clients across the Canadian prairies. My job was to open pathways for more companies and individuals to use our payment methods, which over time, felt very consumeristic and empty. There was nothing tangible I could see at the end of the day that I had done or created. The work didn't feed my passions or link to my core values, nor did it use my best creative strengths.

The more I fought to ignore this misalignment, the more stressed I felt. I tried to compartmentalize and explore passions outside of work, but after devoting so many years to working 50-60 hour weeks, I felt like I didn't even remember what my passions were. By staying in a role that was tightly defined within its own job description, I was limited. Every time I tried to add more creativity or tried to solve problems in a different way, I hit a wall. I was told no. It got to a point when every day was spent in survival mode, going through the motions. I was struggling with sleep, showing signs of depression, and heading toward burnout. Some days, my energy was so low that it was hard to drag myself out of bed. At the end of the week, I felt wrung out like a wet rag. If you've ever felt that way, you understand.

I wanted to do something different but couldn't think of what that was. For me, though, it's never been about the title. I never cared about having the 'VP of such and such' behind my name, even when my peers made me feel like I should care. I had been in sales and marketing roles my entire career, so I felt like the path was already decided for me. What else could I do? Where could I earn as much money so that I wouldn't have to starve? Okay, starving is dramatic, but my husband and I were attached to the lifestyle we had built and didn't want to take a big step backward. I was wearing the golden handcuffs that so many people wear, stuck thinking that the entire world would collapse if I made a change, that I would never be able to earn what I wanted while doing the things I love.

So, how did I get out of this rut? Is this something anyone can do? Absolutely. Here are the five key steps you can take to do the same.

1. **Get clear on what matters to you:**

I had previous studies in yoga philosophy and went back to those teachings to acknowledge that my trapped feelings only existed in my mind. I had to search for what would bring me joy. I started to look at my job and what aspects I did and did not like about my role, company, work environment, and industry. Then, I thought back to when I was younger and felt free from adult obligations like mortgages, saving for retirement, and keeping up with the Jones's. There were activities I did then that brought me joy: running and playing with friends, being outside in nature, getting groups together to build structures, coaching soccer, and leading a public speaking club.

When I married those two lists together, I saw common threads of what fuels my energy and propels me forward without it feeling like work. They all had to do with guiding, teaching, and supporting people. Those were also things I was good at.

It became clear that I had to explore the coaching profession. To validate if that was right, I interviewed two established executive coaches to learn from their experiences – pros, cons, advice, and pitfalls. They were all things I could live with. Soon after, I committed to and enrolled in training. After the first weekend intensive class, I was energized and wanted to take the second level. The more I learned, the more inspired I felt. Six months later, I had completed the course work and was left with the decision of where to go next. I had no idea if it would go anywhere but felt drawn to continue because, in truth, I had wanted to be an entrepreneur my entire life.

All of this happened while I was still working, so I had to find ways to stay motivated. Since I now understood that the people component was what mattered to me the most, this became my focus at work. I minimized emails and started talking on the phone more to get things done. I set little priorities each week to help focus my attention and tried not to worry about perfection.

People talk all the time about taking the leap into entrepreneurship. That's a very narrow view of what it's really like. If you jump off a cliff by yourself with no plan, no contingency, and no support, you're going to foolishly crash.

Your chances of success go up exponentially when you have all of them in place first.

2. **Plan out a roadmap.**

Let's start with the obvious part: money. My training alone was going to cost in the neighborhood of $10,000, and I had to figure out where the money would come from and how to convince my husband it would be a good investment. At that point, I didn't even know if I would make a living from it, but still created a spreadsheet of the payments over time and what income could compensate. Then, thinking about the transition from full-time work with a side business to making it my full-time gig, I had a couple of income scenarios laid out with clear business development plans to get there, based on what I knew so far. Doing this exercise pointed out the gaps.

The second element to plan for was time. With the number of hours I was working, it was an important part of the equation. I planned the time off work for in-person training courses, listed what resources I needed, and scheduled time in my calendar for everything. If you're looking at doing this yourself, you won't know all the variables for your entire future, but you need to at least know the first two to three things and estimate the rest. Then, keep updating and adjusting the plan as you go.

Pick a date. For most people, this is the hardest part because let's face it, life happens! I stalled on picking a date for two years and could not commit myself to the life I wanted out of fear. I wondered if maybe it wasn't the 'right time' because I still lived with those golden handcuffs. Even though my coach training and building community around me was sparking inspiration and movement in my thinking, I was still attached to the habit of how I was living and working at the time. I couldn't see the path forward yet.

The whole world changed for me when one sunny Saturday in July, my husband died from a tragic fall that broke his neck. Suddenly, nothing made sense, and I was completely disoriented, walking around in a dark cloud. I was forced to take time off from work and from everything. I grieved slowly and privately. It's hard for me to tell this story, but it's so important to my journey because it jolted me into focus. It was now all up to me. My future and that of my two-year-old son were all up to me. I had a choice: to keep living exactly the same, go to work, do what I 'had to,' come home, make dinner, watch TV, go to bed dreading the next day, rinse and repeat... aka, live like a zombie. Or I could choose to live differently, with purpose and meaning. I wanted to set an example for my son; that even in the face of hard things like loss, it's possible to feel fulfilled and move forward and that life is meant to be fun!

Initially, I did go back to work, now a widow and single mom. I was even more unfulfilled than before because I was still grieving and felt the work was pointless. It was time to commit to a plan because I had personally experienced how short life really is. My new perspective helped me find the strength to set the exit date. When I say you need a plan, it doesn't stop at just setting the end date for your current situation.

You need to, at least, know the first step. I set a date four months out, stuck to my savings plan, and told myself I would not leave without at least one corporate contract and two private coaching clients, which I already had. I got busy on prospecting and landed a signed contract after three months. When I gave my employer notice after being there for eight years, I didn't know if they were surprised or not. I was proud of myself, though, for hitting my goal - my last day of full-time work was four days before the date I had written down.

3. **Clear the path and start saying 'No.'**

Even before I fully committed to embark on the entrepreneur path, I made accomplishing any goal or new experience a game. My self-declared game rules started by drawing a line down the center of a piece of paper. On the left, I had to write down the goal or experience I wanted and all the things I would say 'Yes' to bring me closer to it. On the right side, I forced myself to list one or more things I would say 'No' to that make room for what I wanted. The no's are the hard part. Here's an example: I wanted to go to Nashville with my marathon-running friend. It was a bucket list trip for me because I love live music. To say 'Yes' to Nashville, I had to say 'No' to some sales-training revenue while I was away and pull money from savings to pay for the trip. Not only that, but I had to spend four nights away from my 3-year-old for the first time ever. I upped the ante, too, by running 10KM in the Rock and Roll marathon, which was a ton of fun! All the positive experiences were well worth the sacrifices.

There have been several sacrifices and compromises to pursue my goals. My family and husband struggled to understand why I would leave a successful job to take on the risk of working for myself. It's not their fault. I kept my inner friction somewhat hidden because even I tried to talk myself out of it for a long time. Eventually, something had to give, and I had to make them understand what I was going through. So, on a relationship level, I had to say 'No' to keeping the peace and ignoring my values and creative needs. Both my husband and my family were risk-averse and fearful that I would fail. I was too, so I had trouble standing my ground. I swallowed my fear and had the difficult conversations to ask for the support I needed to focus and succeed, which weren't all without friction. I had to give up several weekends with my infant son to complete the courses, so they all had to step up and help with childcare. We paid a cleaning lady to come into the house to take the workload off of me. My day job work started to fit into fewer hours because I needed my evenings for homework after my son went to bed. I quite the book club I had been part of with great friends too. There were many other choices I had to make along the way to open up space for me to follow my new vision.

4. **Have a contingency**

Whether the change you are considering is a business or career change, there may be a period of adjustment where you take a dip in earnings or take projects that aren't exactly what you want to do but put you on the right path. During the planning phase, it's important to know your needs, as well as what you are willing and not willing to be flexible on.

I built up a buffer of savings, so I wouldn't make poor decisions out of desperation. Six months of expenses in a savings account, to be exact because I couldn't afford to screw this up. I didn't want to regret leaving my job and jump right back into full-time work for someone else or do projects that pulled me away from my mission. I also calculated minimum project values and translated them into terms of hourly rates. I did this so I wouldn't enter into negotiation and end up resenting the work I was doing for the number of hours it took or the outcomes from that work. One of the projects started out with the work I love to do in creating a cohesive team and improving their empathy and communication among leaders. However, as we continued to work together, I got pulled into other HR tasks that weren't really my strength and didn't pay well for the amount of time and energy I put in. Had I not built up a buffer fund, I would have continued to say 'Yes' to that work for the money and pulled off my true course.

Around this time, one of my mentors suggested a heart vs. money matrix, and I began plotting every project on it. Basically, if it was clear that money was low and I had little love for the work, I had to say 'No' to that too. If values are your compass guiding you forward in the adventurous hike of life, then having a contingency is like the extra clothing you need to weather the hail storms.

As a single mom, everything rests on me. If my business doesn't survive and I can't pay my suppliers and personal bills, it's all on me to fix. I never let it get to that point. I always have a large runway of clients and projects on the go, as well as prospects in the wings. Some people would feel very insecure about having an unpredictable nature to their work and income. For me, it's exciting that I get to be in control of my own schedule and income potential. There's no cap or ceiling on the amount I can make as long as I figure out how to optimize my time.

5. **Find or build support around you**

There is no way I could have made it this far alone. Luckily, I have an amazing core group of friends and a supportive family, but their love and encouragement are biased when it comes to business.

I sought out other entrepreneurs and formed connections with those I respected and admired. A small group of us formed a founders mastermind group, and we still meet every two weeks. Each individual has a different background and experiences from mine. We are at various stages of business, and we all bring unique perspectives. The key agreement is total honesty with a goal of fueling each other's development and success. None of us have a vested interest in each other's business beyond wanting to see each other thrive as humans.

My group is the first to tell me if my idea sucks. I need to hear that. They are also the first to encourage me to do something outside my comfort zone and connect with someone they know who can help me. The group pushed me to set up my first website, they challenged my thinking when I got ready to make a capital investment, and they expected updates when I pursued a new strategic partnership. Having people I declare my goals to, stay accountable to, and share roadblocks we can workshop through together and celebrate successes with is one of the key reasons I kept going.

You need this kind of support if you are planning to make big changes in your life.

All of the many little steps I took brought me to where I am. As I sit in my office with the sun reflecting off my glass-top desk, I appreciate the variety I get to experience in my business and in the life I have created. My team supports business owners and sales leaders to create revenue certainty while also finding meaning from the work they do. Not everyone has the privilege of matching their work to their core values. I feel blessed to do that.

What matters to me is the impact I have on my clients, and that they leave our sessions feeling like they got clarity out of our conversation, from the questions I ask them and the perspective I bring. My commitment to them is there will be no bullshit. That promise matters to me and makes the outcome more impactful, which is why I do what I do.

My clients tell me regularly that I have a positive impact on their lives and the choices they make for themselves. For me, that is the most fulfilling part of my work. One of the entrepreneurs I worked with felt undervalued in her consulting work. After our sessions on the topic, she took action to double her rates on her next contract and aligned with her concern for the planet. Another client had lost the sense of meaning in his role and felt stuck. During our sessions, his focus shifted to exploring what qualities gave him meaning, and two exciting new job opportunities came up.

I designed my business to fit the lifestyle I want instead of the other way around. I live life on my terms, not in terms of somebody else's definition of what it should look like. I finish my meetings every day by 3:30 pm, so I can pick my son up from school. Most working moms don't have the luxury of hearing kids' post-class excitement.

People often ask me what a day in my life looks like, and I'm happy to say that no two days look exactly the same. Here is an example of a real day:

- I started the day with a CEO coaching session
- Planned out my schedule for the next quarter
- Rescheduled meetings to make room to facilitate a new training session
- Had a couple of short phone meetings before going for lunch with a client
- After lunch, I followed up on the status of two proposals
- Then, I got ready to interview a new social media coordinator over coffee at Starbucks. By the time I was done the interview and agreed to hire her, it was time to pick up my son from school.

My days are dynamic, and most of my work can be done from anywhere. My late husband and I had a holiday trailer, and I thought it'd be so cool if I could find a way to work and spend summers at the trailer on a lake with my son. So, every business plan and opportunity I said 'Yes' to have been aligned with the goal of being location-flexible.

I take a minimum of five full weeks of time off every year, I travel, and I ski mid-week when everyone else is at the office. Now that my son is older, we ski together on the weekends as well.

We live in a beautiful four-bedroom house in a sought-after neighborhood in Calgary. My neighbors are doctors, lawyers, pilots, oil and gas executives, CEOs, etc. Most of them are extremely curious about my work and lifestyle because there are less guardrails on my time.

Like I said in the beginning, my story is still being written… Dreams and goals continue to be declared and take shape because of the way I have designed my work around the life I want. I have a lot to be thankful for, and the more I embrace that mindset, the more experiences I find to be grateful for.

I don't have superpowers, but I feel like Wonder Woman on the inside. I wish the same for you.

Chantalle Stott

Chantalle has been an entrepreneur for over 20 years, with the last nine in the coaching industry.

During that time, she built both successful traditional and non-traditional businesses with many lessons, aka failures.

She is passionate about helping people create a business and life that motivates them and gets them out of bed every morning with enthusiasm and joy, supporting their families and their dreams.

She has been married for 22 years and has a full house, with our 22-year-old daughter, pup Monte, kitties Mickey and Maia, our grandpup Nova, and Dalilah, the axolotl.

Fueled by love, gratitude, and food!

Connect with Chantalle:

https://www.facebook.com/chantalle.rocheleaustott

https://www.instagram.com/chantallestott/

https://www.linkedin.com/in/chantalle-stott-bb0a5b68/

Chapter 2

Living in Contrast

By Chantalle Stott

Life is a series of contrasts, and our lives seem to be experienced through extremes.

You can't possibly know the perfect bath temperature unless you've sat in one that was too hot and another that was too cold.

It's through multiple experiences that we discover not only who we are, but we develop our character through varied experiences. Part of this is growing through adversities; our traumas become the building blocks for our life's viewpoint. Each lesson and experience is the foundation of our character.

Without these contrasting experiences, there is no way for us to grow, learn, and become.

Of course, not everyone thinks this way, and I can appreciate that as you are walking through the valley, these statements may not resonate. But I can assure you that on either side of the valley, there is always a hill or mountain, and therefore always the choice and option to reach the peek or summit.

How we interpret our obstacles is infinitely up to us.

We can choose to only see the valley, only feel the rain and stare at the peak thinking that it's way too high or hard…or we can acknowledge that there is beauty in the valley because it is sheltered from the weather by the peaks; that its meadows are rich with color because it is fed by the rain, and if we look and allow ourselves to see its beauty, we would be flooded with the beauty of the valley and inspired by the potential of the peaks.

Each and every one of my experiences has yielded the opportunity for growth. Good or bad, and every time it was up to me to see what I wanted to or see what I was meant to.

Typically, if I missed the lesson the first time, life had a way of coming back around to it until the lesson was learned.

So, what if we took on the attitude of not only accepting but being grateful for the challenges? What if we chose to see and acknowledge that the oak is strong because of the wind?

I truly believe that we are in an obstacles crisis. Not one in which we are facing too many, but one where we just aren't facing enough.

A whole generation of us has been able to navigate our lives without a major catastrophic event. A whole generation has been emotionally, physically, spiritually, and mentally accommodated.

These constant accommodations for everything from our fundamental human rights to our basic feelings have left us weak. We lack the fight in us because we've rarely had to use it. Grit and character are like muscles; they atrophy if left unused.

Great strides in history were made during times when humanity faced great obstacles.

Those obstacles presented us with the opportunity to overcome, strengthen and grow. It's under pressure that a diamond is made…otherwise, all we're left with is coal.

The irony, or better yet, the conflict, is that I wouldn't wish my life's experiences on anyone. Abuse, neglect, homelessness, addiction, violence, and deep mental health issues all before the age of 16 isn't the most efficient personal growth plan, but it was mine.

However, I WOULD wish this level of clarity, self-confidence, self-love, empathy, neutrality, and consciousness on everyone. It didn't come easy, but it was worth every bit of what it took to get here.

I kind of see it as Karma. What is given must be earned. So if I had to have had a front-loaded life of trauma for a long life of joy, then I'm happy to have made the payment in advance.

Not everyone sees it this way. But I do.

I would often get asked how I managed such a positive mindset during difficult times, and my response was always the same, regardless of the magnitude of the struggle:

"I have a phenomenal life. If this is the way Karma wants me to pay it back, then so be it."

It didn't matter if it was emergency life-saving surgery or a major car accident; I saw it as some sort of karmic payment for an amazing life.

Now that was a bit naïve, of course, and I've since realized that I do actually have more control over how I pay things back or forward through how I choose to live my life.

Allowing myself to see things solely from a "cause and effect" standpoint took away my personal responsibility around how I lived my day-to-day life. It negated the basic principle of the Law of Attraction, so I had to reframe things so I could regain some control over how my life turned out and not merely live as if the consequences and my life were all preprogrammed.

Since adopting a life of intentionality and choosing to live in a way that is in the service of others, I have seen and regained my strength and power. I have more control over the outcome than I ever thought possible.

In every struggle I've faced, there has been space for opportunity, love, growth, and joy. Every. Single. One.

As a child, I didn't know it, and when you're being neglected or abused, you're not looking for the silver lining, but it's there.

The thing is, just like Karma, there's no timeline.

The lesson may be directly linked to the obstacle in an obvious way, or it may not come until later in life (or not in this or your lifetime at all). The truth is, some of the obstacles we overcome aren't overcome for just us. We are, after all, part of a collective called humanity, and some of our triumphs are for the benefit of many, not just ourselves.

I could give hundreds of examples throughout history where the sacrifices of one resulted in the benefit for many, but this isn't a political book. Nor is it meant to serve as histology of society and its gains through any individual's work.

This is supposed to be a personal, more biographical account of how my personal obstacles led to my personal triumphs and how I created the opportunity from them. So I'll stick to that; otherwise, a whole book, let alone a single chapter, just couldn't do justice to the strides we've all made as a collective through time.

I can't and honestly don't want to sit here and do an audit of my obstacle to opportunity. It would bore you, I'm sure! So I'll just share a bit about the big rock experiences in my life and how I've been able to create huge benefits and opportunities out of them.

I guess my hope for you is that you'll see how you can potentially reframe some of your past traumas and current obstacles into massive growth opportunities through reading how I chose to implement a growth mindset and surround myself with key relationships. I may not have all the answers, but I hope I can give you a good start.

Have you ever wondered why movies, books, and social media influencers with strong stories of overcoming are so popular?

Relatability. We all yearn to be seen and heard, and even if that's through the eyes and experiences of others, we can relate and therefore feel connected.

We all have a story of overcoming. This just happens to be mine.

I've never really fit in. I've always had an abstract way of looking at life and seemed to feel things deeper than most.

When I was in grade school, my mom managed a Ronald McDonald house where most, if not all, of my friends were, essentially, dying. I spent hours at the hospital with friends and their families, learning about and witnessing the power of the human spirit to overcome. Maybe that's why I've never really found it easy to acknowledge my own struggles as struggles. In comparison to how hard I saw my friends fight to live, anything I experienced just didn't seem to matter as much in contrast. This was the first foundational stone to the mindset that ultimately saved my life.

Even though I faced horrific bullying at school as a result of living in the house and didn't have any friends outside of its walls, I didn't seem to be overly affected by it. The kids used to say and tease me that I had cancer. I had and still have no idea why cancer in particular, but they would act as if I was contagious and would ostracize and bully me. I was demeaned, beaten, and would even get rocks thrown at me as I would enter or leave the school grounds.

I personally found the notion ridiculous. I had spent enough time with the families to know that cancer wasn't contagious and didn't understand why anyone would fear someone with cancer when my friends with it (and other illnesses) were some of the most amazing people I'd ever known. They were so strong and so courageous! Almost superhero-like in their strength and determination. It wasn't until a particularly bad beating at school that my mom finally intervened, but even then, the bullying never ended.

The negative impacts of living in the house did eventually start to show themselves. Losing my friends on a daily or weekly basis, either because they went back home or unfortunately passed away, began to take its toll on my mental health. It affected my mom, too, so she eventually found a new job, and we moved away after about a year or so.

Regardless of any negative impact, it was at the Ronald McDonald House and through those amazing friends and families that I first witnessed the power of a neutral and positive mindset.

Although I didn't really understand its value or how to apply it yet, I can, without a doubt, link those experiences as the fertile time where the seeds of a positive mental attitude were planted. You're forced to look at life through a new lens when you witness a dying child laughing, playing, and consuming life without regret, resentment, or fear.

My "oddness" didn't go away with the move, though. I was still too sensitive, too smart, too annoying, too spirited, too challenging, and too weird for most and continued to experience bullying throughout my academic years. I thought too deeply and was a critical thinker from a young age, which for some reason really irritated my teachers; therefore, I found myself in the corner, in hallways, or in the principal's office more than in the classroom.

Eventually, I even ended up being too much for my mom. My high-spiritedness, coupled with my teenage behaviour, seemed to overwhelm her, so at 13, I went to live with my father in Montreal.

Unfortunately, after being sexually abused by his adult stepson, I found myself homeless and living in a way no one, regardless of age, should live. The labels that I received because of my need to survive haunted me. Slut, whore, skank..., to name a few, began to erode my self-image and dampen my spirit. School became harder to attend, and my life felt like it was slipping into a darkness I feared I'd never be able to escape from.

It was Natasha who saved me. We met through a mutual friend (we didn't go to the same school). She was messy and spirited too. She thought too much and spoke too often, and we spent hours lamenting about things most adults wouldn't even consider! Politics, social behaviours, and feminism all mixed in with the normal musings of most 13-year-olds like boys, sex, whether or not to wear ripped jeans, and how desperate we were to be older! Her family helped me get off the streets, and I stayed with them, on and off, between my Dad's (after he left my stepmom) and their house.

Eventually, I moved back to Ottawa with my Mom, who decided life without me was more difficult than life with me.

Regardless of the obstacles I'd faced, I still couldn't conform. I learned at a young age that standing out always felt better than fitting in.

By high school, I was bullied more than ever and hated more than most. I still can't really account for why, except that I was the one always asking the awkward questions, highlighting the inconsistencies around me, and calling out the mediocrity that I would witness daily. I was labeled as troublesome and disruptive by teachers and mostly annoying by anyone else.

Perhaps my circumstances played a part, just like when I lived at the Ronald McDonald house. I didn't have a normal life. Having already experienced a lifetime of hate and hardship by the age of 16, I just couldn't fit in with the normality of my peers. Their common struggles paled in comparison to what I had seen and endured, and my ability to relate to them was non-existent.

I did have friends, though. Misfits just like me, and even though I didn't see it then, it was through them that I was able to foster my curiosity and (in hindsight) my leadership. It was during my darkest moments after moving from Ottawa to Calgary that I met Christine. She introduced me to Sea Cadets, and that experience, coupled with the amazing support I got, opened me back up to my potential. My self-image grew bit by bit, and with some other key relationships in my life, I was able to pick myself up once again.

Then, in grade 12, I was suspended for writing my Social Studies end of term paper on the Holocaust…from the German perspective.

It didn't win me any points in the friend's department and definitely solidified my position as the troublesome student in the eyes of my teachers and principal. That's probably the first time I ever really remember feeling completely defeated and deeply misunderstood. My intention was to bring depth to the conversation. I knew there was a reason why things happened the way they did. I knew that an entire nation had to have been led to a common belief in order for such atrocities to have been allowed to happen, and I believed it was my responsibility as a critical thinker and budding feminist to ask the hard questions and provide the harder perspective.

That belief wasn't shared, and the fallout from it made me bitter and receded into a place of darkness once again.

Life after high school was filled with everything I dreaded and fought against.

Mediocrity set in as I moved out and joined the cycle of living to work and pay bills. I'd fallen into place, slotted in with the rest, working Monday to Friday, exhausted by nine, and then playing hard on the weekends to make up for the mundane existence I now found myself in. The only things really breaking up the monotony were alcohol, sex, and the odd relationship that inevitably ended in heartbreak.

Yet again, it was a key relationship (which I now refer to as Angel encounters) that saved me from this cycle of self-destruction.

Kathy was just like me. Beautifully broken and wonderfully brave. We ventured through the dark together, making our mistakes and facing our consequences, but eventually, we came out the other side stronger and more poised than ever to build our lives based on the things we actually wanted. Not just the things we were subjected to or told we had to tolerate or normalize.

We both got married and had kids (well, she had kids, I had one), and looking back now, I know that she was the catalyst to my rebirth into who I am today.

With every obstacle or unsurmountable hardship I faced, it was a key relationship that helped me overcome. I never truly walked this path alone, even when I felt like I was. The universe was always by my side, conspiring for my success. I guess I always kind of knew it, and that's why I never gave up. I knew that despite being hated by so many, I would eventually be loved by even more.

I didn't think I could account for where that deep routed belief came from, but through reflection and, in part, through writing this chapter, I realized that the seed that was planted so long ago. Planted by all those amazing kids and families fighting the impossible had finally taken root sometime in middle school and just continued to grow from there.

It was the most difficult and darkest days that laid the groundwork for some of my greatest accomplishments.

Being neglected and abandoned led to my deep and unshakable ability to love. Through this, I have built some of the most significant relationships of my life. Today I have a rich and full circle of friends and family by choice who have and continue to support me through life's ups and downs.

Being a sexual abuse survivor has allowed me to be more relatable to others. It has helped me to earn the trust of other survivors so that I can help them overcome their own demons and dark pasts. It's afforded me the privilege to walk through life with them and support them so they, too, could become major impactors in their own ways.

Being hated grew my empathy and compassion. I began to be able to see that other people's hatred has little to do with me (or anyone else for that matter) and more to do with their own hurt and deep-seated need to be loved. As my empathy grew, so did my neutrality. And once again, my ability to see things from the perspective that few ever do lead to my ability to elevate people to their highest potential and out of a pattern of hate and negative behaviours.

Being emotionally abused has allowed me to see through false love and to find true, unconditional love that has led to the most amazing and fruitful marriage with the most amazing man. He's my best friend and sees me and accepts me in a way I never thought possible.

Being ostracized forced me to find my people. The ones making waves of change in every aspect of life and who call me to face the uncomfortable for the greater good of all. They're the misfits and game-changers that make history and leave lasting legacies for future generations to benefit from. They are the people I admire and aspire to be.

Last but certainly not least, being different has led to a full and abundant life.

I didn't stay in a cycle of living to work. I quickly learned that I make a terrible employee anyway, and chances are if I tried to conform, I'd just be living the same cycle of disconnect over and over again. No matter how hard I tried, I had to face the truth. I was never going to fit in, and honestly, I was never meant to.

In every situation and with every obstacle I've faced, there's one common theme that got me through. The opportunities, the overcoming, the healing all came from one thing... Relationships.

The way I not only survived but thrived was through my ability to connect and my willingness to accept help.

If not for key relationships throughout my life, I know for a fact that I wouldn't be where I am today and may not even be at all.

Every single one of the opportunities that have come my way has come through authentic and meaningful connections, and I believe this is the ultimate key to success.

There are no such things as "self–made." This idea is part of the reason why I think so many people fail and feel so alone. They try and "go it" by themselves.

Fact is, the overly romanticized idea of the "lone wolf" has long been debunked. Lone wolves die. It's that simple. Basic evolution and primal survival have been shown to be achieved through community and collaboration. Wolves are pack animals, and so are humans.

It's through key relationships that I learned how to see the world from a more positive lens, to always look for the rainbow (i.e., relationship/help), and to work smarter through collaborations.

Everything up until this point has helped me build a life where the work is the living, and the living is the work. A life where who I am and the values I hold matter, where my character trumps anything else.

I get to live a value-driven life on my terms, and, through it all, I've learned the best life is one lived in community, in the service of others, and with the people who see you for who you are.

I get to live a life without compromise because I never did. Conformity isn't the key to success. It may be the path of least resistance but remember, without pressure, the diamond cannot be formed...and who wants just a pile of coal anyway?

Dorothy Briggs

Dorothy Briggs Is the founder and publisher of Womanition® Magazine, a venture so successful that it quickly led to an entire network of Womanition® Connect Groups throughout the province uplifting and empowering women in countless communities, plus continues to educate, motivate, and inspire businesswomen, through the thriving Womanition® 6 Pillars of Womanition.

Connect with Dorothy:

www.womanition.com

www.vavasaur.com

www.facebook.com/womanitionconnect

Chapter 3

A Legacy in Perseverance

By Dorothy Briggs

Believe it or not, there was a time when the concept of mentoring was lost on me. In my early unenlightened days, I would never have dreamed of asking for advice myself, so why would I tell anyone what I was thinking or planning and offer guidance to them? I was always sure someone would steal my ideas and take the credit. Where would that then leave me?

Today, as the proud creator of the *Womanition* "empire," consisting of six pillars of opportunity designed to unite, promote and empower businesswomen and entrepreneurs, the advancement of mentorship is one of my primary passions. It gives me immense joy watching women change and grow their businesses from the smallest start-up into a thriving, profitable ventures. I am honored to be a part of their success.

Of course, now, I understand the truth. There's no need to fear competition. Abundance is limitless. The endless flow of ideas and ingenuity is stimulated, not stymied, by the give and take associated with collaboration. Paying it forward doesn't diminish what you have. Instead, it ultimately increases your rewards.

In fact, the *Womanition Mentorship Program* is my own way of paying it forward and an accessible, supportive forum where up-and-coming entrepreneurs can benefit from the experiences of a select team of seasoned business women, all inspired to share their knowledge and expertise. I knew that offering such an advantage to our annual round of protégées would save them years of needless floundering, propelling them forward, instead, much more rapidly towards business success. I want to teach them all the pitfalls before they fall into the "pit." As the program manager and a mentor myself, all protégées can call on me at will while currently in the program, and, in subsequent years, my door is always open to them as well.

My extensive "people" experience gives me tremendous insight into the effective pairing of a protégée with their most suitable mentor. My process is such that I clearly emphasize to the protégées that acceptance into the program is a true privilege. Since mentors are putting in time and energy sharing their gifts for no financial recompense, the protégées must be respectful of the program parameters in terms of attendance, punctuality, and the completion of assignments. If individuals are not honouring the process, they will be asked to leave.

Since mentors donate their time, they should strive to maximize their effectiveness, primarily by being very clear in their instructions and expectations. I let mentors and protégées agree on how they will interact, by phone, Skype, or face-to-face. Personally, I feel that, by conversing in person, you can convey so much more information through facial reaction, body language, and voice inflection.

Experience has taught me that most people don't really want to change, even if they think they do. They want the ideal of business success, yes, but they don't care to do the deep, difficult, "face-your-fears" work that it takes. They're too comfortable to leave their comfort zone. So, you end up with 20% of the people doing 80% of the work. This is where my mentorship program truly works. If you do what it takes to stay in the program, you can't help but be pushed out of your comfort zone, refreshed by all the new ideas.

Women tend to be too self-effacing, which, unfortunately, is a serious challenge to their advancement. Devoting all their time, energy, and money to the needs of others, they put themselves and their own needs last. There is a reason that the airline safety protocol instructs you to put your own mask on first before helping others.

The same holds true in entrepreneurship. If you don't help yourself first, spend that time, energy, and money on your own business, then how do you expect to reach your goals? If you don't give to yourself, you'll never be in the position to be able to give back to others. Of course, you need to balance work and family, not seriously sacrifice one at the expense of the other. If your business needs something to succeed, you have to be ready to step up to the plate.

To me, the mark of a serious business person is a clear respect for other people's time. Despite the variety of perspectives on the importance of punctuality, the fact remains that the accepted business standard is to act with consideration and integrity, in that when you agree on a designated appointment time or deadline, you honour that agreement. It is disrespectful to repeatedly be late without notice, giving the impression that your colleagues' time is less valuable than yours. I would say emphatically to any aspiring business person that you should make punctuality a priority!

Is there a legitimate excuse for tardiness? In special circumstances, yes. However, I remember my childhood Girl Guide motto: be prepared. I was taught that whatever you need to do, you make sure you can do it. Again, it's a matter of integrity. Any number of things can happen, so be prepared for every contingency. Make sure if Plan A flops, your backup Plan B comes into effect, and then your Plan C, if all else fails. For the most part, punctuality is within your control if you plan ahead the way you should in a business situation. Conducting yourself accordingly shows a respectful, responsible attitude towards your business and your clients.

Our end-of-program mentorship protégée survey provides the frank and uncensored feedback I need to ensure the ongoing effectiveness of this quality experience. Should you, the reader, know of any businesswoman seeking to learn more about working with a mentor, I would be happy to provide information.

I wouldn't be where I am today without the encouragement and support of my own long-time mentor, Donna Worthington, who continues to push me out of my comfort zone. I truly respect her brilliant mind. Our collaborative projects always succeed because we devise a plan, and then we work the plan. This kind of focus and determination never fails.

In contrast, I think I just assumed, in my younger years, that I had to go it all alone. Small wonder, growing up in a middle-class, blue-collar family, daughter of a violent, mentally ill, alcoholic father and a stay-at-home mom. Those were dark times, even after my father left. My mother, forced into the working world out of necessity, could barely afford to feed the family.

I know I must have inherited my indomitable sense of inner pride and strong work ethic from my mother, who refused to go on welfare despite our debilitating financial situation. It was a questionable decision, as I see it now, considering that negating outside help is, in essence, obstructing the flow of abundance pouring in from the universe, the abundance that is your birthright. It took me a very long time to learn that lesson. I've made lots of mistakes that cost me time and money because, like my mother, I was tenaciously adamant about doing it my way.

It seemed to me that I was always the different one out of all my family and friends. I was always so bold and confident in my attempts to do whatever I felt compelled to do in business and life. If I believe it works, it's going to work. If I make up my mind that it's going to happen, it will happen. Some of my attempts have succeeded, and, naturally, some of them appear to have failed, but I never give up. I hold true to my vision. It is not despite these failures, but *because* of them, that I have achieved my success.

My original aspirations for *Womanition* have flourished beyond my wildest dreams. When I pushed aside my self-doubts and published my first issue of the *Womanition Magazine,* an annual publication showcasing women entrepreneurs, I never imagined that, a few short years later, I would have a trophy case of gold and platinum awards for production, design, layout, special edition and advertising.

My vision was all about women building communities *of* women *for* women. It has led to the growing number of monthly *Womanition* networking meetings in the Calgary and Edmonton regions, featuring fascinating, educational presentations from speakers who are part of our diverse and thriving membership of over a thousand women.

Designed to further the business acumen of women entrepreneurs in and outside the *Womanition* family, the widely acclaimed *BizBrigade Leadership Conference* came into being. An informative, motivational experience, this event offers a selection of the best and brightest member speakers sharing their wisdom and expertise.

What better way to distinguish these business luminaries than through our *SuPEARLative Awards Program*? This gala ceremony honours not just my amazing *Womanition* "wonder women" but their worthy counterparts representing women in the workforce province-wide. As an inventive twist on the typical awards trophy, our winners are awarded a stunning piece of pearl jewelry to commemorate their outstanding achievements.

Most recently, I launched an online-only professional profile opportunity complete with a photo and bio. Now, our *Business Briefs* are steadily gaining popularity.

I credit the success of my beloved *Womanition* to this proven formula comprised of these six pillars, which, of course, include the aforementioned *Womanition Mentorship Program* as well. Intended to enlighten the business stars of tomorrow, the program provides valuable insight on an array of topics, including finance, sales, leadership, confidence, marketing, branding, relationship building, and so much more.

My goal is to teach this formula to a personally chosen team of high-energy *Womanition* leaders in each major city across North America and beyond in order to build a prosperous and supportive collaborative network of women business leaders worldwide. With this in mind, I am looking for the right women to share my dream; like-minded women gifted in sales who love working with other women.

Make no mistake, the *Womanition* brand, my little empire that I have built to champion women entrepreneurs, has only just begun. I have always been one to reinvent myself, to seek out new opportunities, but within the *Womanition* realm, I have found my true passion, helping women in business to help each other.

In the spirit of paying it forward, I have recently founded a non-profit organization called the *Association of Community Engaged In Sharing* (ACES). When our project is finalized, we will be funded by grants allowing us to achieve our mandate to mentor immigrant women from all over the world. I admire immigrants because they are here to make our lives better, as well as their own. Immigration is so important. We live in the best country in the world, open to new people and new experiences!

I intend to first meet with these women to determine their individual needs, along with those of their community. ACES' goal is to help immigrant women learn the strategies they need to join the business world. They will be taught skills such as English language proficiency, resume writing, the job application process, how to dress professionally, and show confidence and leadership in their interviews. We want to help them fit easily into our society so they feel comfortable in their new country. Without compromising their way of life, we want to mentor them in embracing ours. I trust that working through ACES to make a positive difference in the lives of these brave women will be my legacy.

I am a publisher, an author, a visionary, and a connector, the driving force behind a growing community of women leaders who help each other, learn from each other, and do business with one another, celebrating their successes together. What's my secret? Irrational optimism! Irrational optimism is the belief that what you intend will manifest itself, that what you begin will succeed, despite all evidence to the contrary. It's a trait found in every successful person, and I possess it in abundance!

Now, I've learned to spread my irrational optimism among others, share my vision, and compel other like-minded women to rally behind my community. This, in turn, so enriches their lives that, in gratitude, they're inspired to enrich the lives of others. In paying it forward, everyone is blessed full circle.

Miracles really do happen when you show up. I cannot count the times I have reluctantly dragged myself to some meeting or event, only to discover the greatest gift, an unexpected connection to amazing new people who, ultimately, have helped me change and grow. My passion is to help other women succeed in *their* passion, whatever their chosen contribution to the world may be in business and life.

Hopefully, the women who read the stories of the unique individuals within this book will be empowered to feel "irrationally optimistic" themselves as they walk their unique path to success, focused unwaveringly on their own goals.

We "*Womanition*" women are here for you, and we care.

You must believe in yourself.

I know in my heart and soul that, no matter how it seems on the outside, no matter what adversity stands in my path, if I believe in something and take it on, it will work. I picture it gloriously succeeding in my mind, all up and running just the way I want it to be before I even start.

There's truly more than enough for everyone.

It's crazy how some people are jealous of other people's success. How counter-productive! The truth is that just because one person has a lot, it doesn't mean that they are taking anything away from you. All you desire is right there, yours for the having. However, you must do the work to receive it.

If those who are misguided could only realize that those successful people worked their hearts out to get what they now have, even gave up time with family, friends, and partners to pursue their goals and visions. Success is earned. I believe that it's easy to judge others when the reality is that many people are too unmotivated to get out there and make the effort to get what they want. It's WORK, ladies! If you're not where you want to be in life, seek the help of an expert to help you get there. Of course, you'll have to pay for it, but see it as the best investment you will ever make in yourself and your future.

Never give up – persistence pays!

Even when things looked bleak, I still had faith that my efforts would pay off, and they did. It's been proven to me time and time again. Sometimes, things didn't always turn out the exact way I wanted. In the end, however, I was happy with the result. For further enlightenment, I suggest that you read *Think and Grow Rich* by Napoleon Hill.

Fran Dunscombe

Fran Dunscombe is a hypnotherapist and coach from the UK and has been living in Calgary, AB, Canada, since 2014.

She spent 15 years successful in corporate only to realize that it was not the space where she could be fulfilled. Her challenges with low confidence, self-criticism, and judgment led her to seek a hypnotherapist's help, which inspired her to re-train and follow a new path.

She is a voice for people that haven't experienced major trauma but still feel stuck and blocked and can't work out why or how to get out of the mud. Her empathic and fun approach helps her clients understand themselves with more love and compassion while opening up the door to possibilities that didn't seem available before.

She's a nature-loving, yoga-practicing, fun, and adventure seeker desiring to live life to its fullest.

Friendship and relationships are significant values of hers, and she's grateful for the people in her life, especially Jessica Trozzo and her beloved fiancé, Ben Richardson, who both offered encouragement and guidance in writing her chapter for this book.

Connect with Fran:

fran@trueinnerconnection.com

Chapter 4

The Joy of Overcoming & Being Wrong

By Fran Dunscombe

I am incredibly grateful for the depth of how wrong I have been.

Throughout my journey in life and business, I am constantly learning how wrong I've been about how much I can overcome. When I reflect, it feels as though the universe has been conspiring to make me wrong (in the best way possible!) to prove to me that I am, indeed, an overcomer.

Without my being wrong, I certainly wouldn't be writing this, and you wouldn't be reading this because more fear of judgment would have kept me trapped in a little box!! If I had followed through on my perceptions about myself during some of my lowest times, such as when I have believed "I don't really deserve to be here" and "the world and all the people I know would be better off without me," then I simply wouldn't be here at all.

In 2020, during the height of the pandemic, I got very reflective (there's nothing like a pandemic to trigger some deep self-inquiry) and had an epiphany on this idea. I realized I had been wrong about a lot of things, and through this reflection, I am happy to say I am100% ok with being wrong! But it has been a process, slowly and gradually, and I had to take a step back and realize.

After noting how wrong I had been about many things, it occurred to me how all too often, we get stuck in our heads and hold ourselves back in life because we are convinced by the stories we tell ourselves. On top of that, we don't often take the time to really recognize our growth and the mountains we have already climbed.

For most of my life, I've been incredibly self-critical, self-deprecating, and (on some level) taken pleasure in putting myself down. It's often said we are our own worst critics; I know this to be true for myself and for many other people. We see it in each other easily; think of all those times you might have said, 'don't be so hard on yourself to a friend, family member, or even a *complete stranger*, but we don't see the same in ourselves quite so easily. We get captivated and controlled by the stories we tell ourselves, and all too often, our stories tell us we're wrong, so why bother, and so we never get started. It's as if we conjure and cast spells that are often so deep, so sneaky, and insidious that we can't see them for the bullshit and fallacy that they are.

My self-criticism and assumption of being in the wrong were often wrapped up under the guise of realism. I consider myself to be a very realistic and logical person. The problem with this 'realism' was that it was very limiting; it kept holding me back, sometimes it stopped me completely- I didn't need to overcome; I was safer if I stayed put. I put myself in a box that was as equally comfortable as it was uncomfortable. It meant I knew where I was at with life, but on the flip side, my heart desired more from life. This disconnect meant I would go through periods of feeling stuck, lonely, and depressed, not really knowing why. I'd reflect on childhood and couldn't see it. I had a 'normal' upbringing, no abuse, and I felt loved, for the most part. There was sibling rivalry, teachers shaming me, but surely that couldn't explain the degree of my self-sabotaging. So, what was it? Why? Oh, why, oh why did I feel this way? The only conclusion to be reached at this point in time was that I was broken.

I had been spinning a story since I was five years old that there was something wrong with me, that I was a misfit. I can remember a few specific experiences at that age which generated a lot of shame and self-judgment that I was wrong. This judgment only got worse when I got into my teens. I would have flashbacks and bad dreams, and I remember saying to myself, "you can't ever amount to anything," while at the same time imagining a press conference rolling out where I was being publicly shamed. This fear caused me to play small and step away from my power instead of into it and not face challenges head-on.

Being a *"good girl"* was important to me, and the idea of being shamed and called out for being bad or doing something wrong was terrifying for me. I learned this way of being in the family dynamic. I was raised with a strong moral foundation, not religious but, nonetheless, a clear indication of what is right and wrong and that being a good girl was an expectation, at least in the eyes of my parents; my child-self interpreted this to mean 'in order to be loved, I must be a good girl. I also felt the need to keep up with my big brothers. As a little one at that time, I completely idolized and would do just about anything to hang out with them. My desire to be good kept me in an unhappy relationship for too long because I had thought that you were only supposed to have sex with one person. After leaving that unhappy relationship with a lot of self-judgment and self-loathing for how I showed up in it, I declared that I would never get married and doubted I would ever meet anyone special because, well, no one would love someone as fucked up as me.

At 17, I developed an eating disorder that, although triggered by words, was an expression of my anxiety which had existed for a long time before I was triggered. The huge thing this experience taught me was the incredible power of words; words triggered my eating disorder and started to pull me out of it. I blocked it out of my mind for a while. Denial is a sneaky bugger, but I can recollect the specific conversation with a friend at college, after which I made the decision not to eat. My interpretation of the words turned what was likely intended as a compliment into an eating disorder. On the flip side, a conversation with a friend a year or so later started to pull me out of it; she was relaying something traumatic she had been going through, and I had this sudden, very daunting realization that I had been utterly and completely self-absorbed, wrapped up in my anxieties and obsessions. It was a very humbling moment for me. Words have power and influence, and we should never underestimate the power of words.

So how is it that a young girl from Shrewsbury who thought she wasn't clever, likable, or loveable, and believed that she was a misfit who couldn't amount to anything, become educated, develop long-lasting friendships, have a happy long term relationship, a successful career then transition into business ownership?

I began a journey of healing and introspection, which has bought awareness of these stories I have been spinning and an understanding of how it was formed. This understanding has enabled me to be more compassionate to myself and the world around me. Now I know that everyone is going through a struggle, even people who appear well put together. Everyone has challenges and obstacles to overcome, everyone can be right, and everyone can be wrong, and it's ok. This knowing brings about humility and compassion for myself and those around me; it enables me to be gentler with myself because rather than thinking I am broken, I can see that I am just being human. I don't have to be and cannot possibly be perfect. It's a simple but profound realization to have!

Despite my insecurities and fears, there has been a part in me that knew I had to push through my comfort zone and adopt a "do it anyway" mentality, even if I thought I was wrong to think someone like me deserved the things desired in my heart. I knew I had to push through it before I performed in gymnastics before I went to university when I was searching for a good job, and I knew if I was to leave my corporate job, I was surely going to have some serious discomfort to push through. I knew I was going to try and prove myself wrong; about all the insecurities that came from these shifts, I longed for. I remember a specific conversation with a friend before going to university where I was expressing my anxieties, and she asked, "Well if you feel like that, why are you going?" I remember replying, "I'm scared, but something tells me it will be good for me, and I have to do it." I was right, I didn't know what the lesson was at the time, but I needed to learn that I could stand on my feet and support myself and that I did have the ability to make friends. Adopting a "do it anyway" attitude is absolutely essential to making it in business, too; you have to be willing to try and take action. Prove yourself right… or wrong. They are both 100% ok- they will each teach you something if you look for the lessons and those lessons ultimately lead you to overcome your unique personal challenges to allow your growth to be its fullest.

One of the things that helped me in my journey of overcoming is being open to feedback. That's not to say my initial reaction is always positive (I'm the type of person that can and often will feel defensive initially), but having the ability to set the reaction aside and reflect on feedback and to self-assess has served me well. Sometimes the feedback from interviews really hurt, but it needed to be heard. In time I overcame my defensive mindset and listened to the feedback for what it was. This, in turn, led to a great interview at a job I really wanted, and *this*, in turn, landed me that job!! After landing the job, I was met with new challenges that also required my desire to learn to overcome them. To become competent at my job, I had to go back to university and get a master's degree while working full time; I had to learn to navigate meetings with mostly men twice my age which felt intimidating, especially since I hardly ever felt like I knew what I was talking about, and I had to regularly deliver presentations which scared the hell out of me (hello imposter syndrome). When I made my way to overcome my fear of judgment and recognized that I was competent (bye-bye imposter syndrome), I noticed that my femininity and ability to listen were a gift and enabled me to handle tough negotiations without having to be bolshy or rude. I was also forced to implement healthier boundaries and not say yes to everything, and I discovered that my people-pleasing tendency was a gift because I could often pre-empt how the other person might feel and deliver my boundaries in a caring way, which made confrontation way less scary and easier to do (more overcoming).

My journey into hypnotherapy was a big turning point for me and a huge factor in overcoming obstacles going forward. Having guidance and not just trying to figure it out by myself and having someone to elicit the answers from me boosted my learning process; it was like getting a major download and upgrade at the same time. Awareness would come to me at light speed, and the cogs in my brain started connecting and clicking into place. I first went to see a hypnotherapist because of my fears and imposter syndrome at work. Delivering presentations was a huge trigger of anxiety for me. I remember showing up to my first session sitting in the chair awkwardly, practically clutching the chair in fear of what was about to happen and what I might say or be made to do, but I was soon at ease and had the most incredible experience. I am not just saying this because this is what I do now, but if you have not tried it and other things aren't working, then give it a go!! In one session, I remember coming out of it feeling unstoppable; it was amazing! Mostly to see how quickly emotions and thoughts can shift when we allow ourselves to be open and get honest. In a short space of time, my anxiety had shifted, and I was delivering presentations with more ease and confidence and even making jokes. Whereas before, I would shake like a leaf and scramble through voice shaking the whole time. Result!

Fast forward a few years, and I have moved to Canada with my beloved, I felt confident in my job, and I was met with a new challenge. This career thing was no longer feeling fulfilling! I desired something that felt like it gave back and didn't make me feel like a number on a sheet. I got curious. I took yoga teacher training, and it reminded me of my interest in matters related to the mind. I got more curious; I delved into hypnotherapy. It turns out it blew my mind!!!! I was able to harness the power I witnessed that day I had my first session and gift it to others. Since then, I have taken various trainings in hypnotherapy, meditation, NLP, and coaching, and I have worked with some amazing therapists and coaches who have got me honest about my story about my heart's desires and taught me how to help other people. Talk about overcoming! If I could harness the power of that day on my own, who cared if I was wrong or right. I can overcome anything; I can do anything, be anything, and have the life I want.

I am incredibly grateful for my journey and learnings through yoga. My yoga teacher training made me curious to explore other healing avenues, and the facilitator and people I took the training were the sweetest people to journey with. I was slightly cynical before I started yoga teacher training, as I wasn't really open to the spiritual side or energetic side of it. It kind of sounded like bull shit to me, but I knew it made me feel good, so I followed that thought. It turns out I was wrong again, and I opened up to some new ideas. Instead, I connected to myself on a deeper level. It was in this space that I learned that my negative ego was as huge as it was limiting. It was also here that I discovered what I could only describe as a spiritual connection. I have come to realize I believe in something bigger than me; it's something that I don't really understand or can put words to other than "the great unknown" or using the words of Queen (the band) 'it's a kind of magic"!! It has opened up a curiosity in me to keep exploring, overcoming, and fully allowing myself to be as ok with being wrong as I am about being right about my judgments on new and scary things. The best thing is it has allowed me to get to know myself better and to trust in life.

Not only has becoming a hypnotherapist and coach affected me in my work life, but personal wins have been huge, too, especially in my romantic relationship. It turns out I was wrong about not being loveable, and I did open up to the commitment of marriage. In fact, I was exceptionally lucky to find an incredible man (he told me while writing this, he would prefer it if I refer to him as a spunk-filled god of a man, hehe ☺) in 2005 who I am still in love with to this day. However, we didn't always recognize how lucky we were and have had some mini break-ups a few times. Having met so young, it was hard not to wonder from time to time if the grass was greener. Now we find ourselves so grateful to have found something so deep, so young. In a relationship, we often forget that both parties show up with their own pains and BS, so like a dance, we must learn to navigate all of that. Collectively in a relationship, you both have to learn to be right and wrong, and the best of it is you have to help each other overcome. We have both learned to be more open and honest about our needs and desires and control defensive reactions, and learn from listening to each other. We operate now more like a team than ever before and continue to grow together.

I'm truly honored that I get to help people and give them the same gifts that I received. It gives me the chance to live in accordance with my values. It's committed me to understand myself more and to, keep nourishing and developing my relationships.

Challenges continue to arise…all the time!! Business ownership has taught me that all routes have challenges, and the key is to be a committed learner and to find ways to be happy, now, at this moment. Life is only ever happening now, and happiness cannot be reserved only for when all of the stars align. Happiness, if we see it right, is like the wind- it is free and can travel anywhere and everywhere. I know I am not wrong about that.

I have also learned to embrace my emotions. Modern society and, to a large degree, the personal growth industry give this impression that we are supposed to feel good all the time. I believe this to be misguided as it denies the gift of learning from overcoming the really uncomfortable stuff. So many of us (myself included for the longest time) avoid looking at the uncomfortable stuff, not realizing that embracing our emotions, all of them good or bad, seemingly right or seemingly wrong, and learning from them, allowing them to flow, provides permission to be in our humanness, which, in turn, leads to a feeling of more wholeness within ourselves where we experience more moments of joy and fulfillment.

Something else I have learned as a business owner is to have your own definition of success. My linear view was success equals a full-time client base and income. Questioning whether this is really true has bought a new insight to me, and that shows that this rigid definition I had was wrong. I notice that success is subjective. Some people truly love having a job and what it can bring them; they do things on the side for free because they don't need the money or believe in charging, and they assist others in experiencing the pure joy of helping another human being grow. It's so easy to whip out the giant measuring stick and start measuring yourself against someone else's definition of success and impose self-judgment. We are unique people with individual values, and we create our own definitions.

Above all this, I found that had it not been for my struggle with my confidence, self-worth, and imposter syndrome, I would not have sought the healing I needed and would not have ended up discovering a path to a life that I feel truly passionate about. So in a beautifully funny kind of way, I'm grateful for my challenges, for them opening up the door and making me see how wrong I really was about myself and how much I can overcome.

Now I have a much more optimistic view of the future. I look forward to the life I am building with my fiancé and puppy and to seeing how we continue to grow and what we can achieve. I know little 5-year-old me and 17-year-old me would be quite surprised and proud of how far we have come.

My hope for you as a reader of this is that you regularly take the time to acknowledge your growth. It can be too easy to ignore the internal magic that is always happening, even when external circumstances may not have changed significantly yet!! The thing to realize is those internal wins are the catalyst for everything else to change.

Your struggle is the path to your greatness and will open up your gifts. All hero's journeys begin with obstacles to overcome.

I hope to be a voice for people that have had the good fortune to have not experienced major trauma yet still feel blocked and confused. I want you to know it's ok; it doesn't matter if you are always right or always wrong; keep going. You will not be stuck forever.

With Love and Happiness,

Fran

Holly Blazina

Holly Blazina is an Ayurvedic gut health specialist, Yogini, and flamenco guitarist who found her kryptonite in chronic fatigue, candida, food sensitivities, and insomnia. She spent nearly 25 years figuring out how to get her life back and now mines that experience to help her clients get rapid results. Now, she's a creative powerhouse and healer in her 50s with energy to burn.

Holly solves bloating, heartburn, and IBS with her unique Gutsy Type method. Transform the emotions behind YOUR digestive struggles with her comprehensive but straightforward program, 1:1 consultations, and Gutsy Yoga, her online member program.

Connect with Holly:

https://www.biggutsylife.com

https://www.facebook.com/groups/biggutsylife

https://gutsytypequiz.com

Chapter 5

Do You Want a Big Gutsy Life?

By Holly Blazina

I've never had a job. The truth is, I've never wanted one; I'm just not wired that way.

Before I finished high school, I knew I wanted to be a musician. My parents believed totally in letting me make my own choices and my own mistakes, yet my Dad was hedging on fully supporting my decision to go study music at university. The turning point came when I told him I was practicing 5 hours a day for my audition; he sat me down for one of the shortest conversations we've ever had:

Dad: You know that artists don't make a lot of money, right?

Me: Yes, I know.

Dad: Do you know that sometimes they have a hard time even paying their bills?

Me: Yes, I know.

Dad: And you want to play music?

Me: Yes.

Dad: Ok, then.

My plan was to get a degree in classical guitar performance. My real love was flamenco, but I knew I was on my path. I didn't know how challenging it was going to be, but I knew I wasn't going to have a problem with money. I decided to teach on my own after working in a studio where I wasn't getting fully compensated for all of the work I was doing there. There I was, in my second year of university in the late 1980s, when the minimum wage was $3.85 an hour, and I was making $25. Although I took it for granted then, getting students by word of mouth was the easiest thing in the world. The truth is, it's still one of the best ways to get clients!

When I graduated (after seven long years), I filled my studio with over 30 new students in a matter of 2 months. Again, word of mouth, a classified ad in a community newsletter, a little creative visualization, and presto, I had consistent income straight out of the gate. And I was only working part-time.

Community equals customer retention. My school ultimately converted from all classical students to flamenco. The first time one of my students asked to learn dance accompaniment, I knew it would become a group program because it's SO much fun to play with dancers!

I had no idea the students would become friends and keep taking lessons because they enjoyed playing and learning together. Looking back on it, the part that excited me the most was that I set it up because I loved it myself and wanted to share the experience. As a rebel, I can only commit to things when I'm a "Hell, Yes!"

Rewinding back to when I was in university, I'd noticed somewhere along the line that I was exhausted. My memory of this was getting off the bus several blocks from home with my guitar and books, not knowing how exactly I was going to get home. My only choice was to put one foot in front of the other and do it. I was only in my 20s, and I knew I should have had the energy to burn, but I didn't.

I booked an appointment with a naturopath, who informed me that I had candida - a yeast overgrowth in the intestinal tract - along with a host of food sensitivities. The recommendation was a diet to eliminate everything that was feeding the yeast, including dairy, wheat, sugar, vinegar, alcohol, and all processed foods. Yikes!!

It would be ages before I saw the light at the end of a long tunnel. It was the beginning of doing all my own cooking or paying the price. Rather than tell my partner I couldn't always cook to his preferences, I did it all while being relentlessly tired.

This went on for several years. The worst part was that the damn diet didn't actually make me feel better, but when I 'cheated,' I felt hungover for at least a full day. I wasn't living soulfully; I was just running nonstop in a hamster wheel. At one point, my aunt called me up to have a serious talk about workaholism. She could see that what I was doing wasn't sustainable - and my health didn't seem to be getting any better.

One day, a friend called to invite me to a free yoga class, which was on every Friday at a local studio. It was like a weekly oasis, and it became a standing date.

I'm not sure which came first, whether I started doing a few yoga poses before bed, or whether I started noticing that my food hangovers weren't lasting as long after our weekly restaurant meal. But I knew yoga was working its magic when I could sleep 10 hours and wake up feeling rested and ready to start the day.

I'd gotten into a rhythm with my food prep, and it was feeling more natural. I also had a bit of newfound flexibility with food; I made a point of ordering whatever I wanted at our weekly dinner out and then returning to my healthy foods the next day without much fuss.

I'd also connected with a flamenco guitarist who'd recently moved to my locale. Here's the thing: I'd wanted to study flamenco before I even knew what it was. I'm not even kidding! When I look back at my introduction to classical guitar, it was the Spanish sounds that drew me into that art form, and my secret thought was, "This isn't quite IT, but it's close!" So I'd already planned to start studying flamenco the minute I was done with my university courses - in fact, I'd very nearly quit school and left for Spain before finishing my degree. But then I met someone, so I didn't... Which is another story.

For me, studying flamenco was exactly like being in love. You know how when you meet someone new, and you think of them as soon as you wake up in the morning? That was me. I'd plan my day around flamenco. People still comment on how much flamenco lights me up!

I wasn't being disciplined; my reverence was absolute without obligation. And let me say, you'll hardly find a more technically demanding art form on the planet. I didn't have a care in the world about how much I sucked at it. I just knew I was home, and I was hungry to engage with it at every opportunity. Part of my instruction was to listen to recordings my teacher provided. I did this all day long, anywhere I could. I was never without a tune or a rhythm.

I was so ALIVE in a way I'd never felt before. Flamenco is a bit like the blues in its sentiment. The Gypsies are an oppressed people, and I related to that emotionally. It's funny how music that can be so gut-wrenchingly sad can be so uplifting. For me, it truly was. It provided me with a place to put all the feelings left over from a very stressful childhood that I didn't know what to do with. Being the creative powerhouse that I am, this flow of energy is critically important for me. Yes, the art form is demanding, and yet, I felt my creative energy truly MOVING for the first time in my life.

I was in a solid groove, my learning curve was steep, and I was all-in like I'd never been before in my life. I was starting to perform, and I was discovering things about myself as a learner that helped me come into my own. While in university, I'd experienced debilitating stage fright, and everything I'd learned there was little more than a workaround, a way of counteracting the fear but not really dealing with it. Of course, it didn't help that perfectionism abounds in the classical world, which fed my own issues in an unwholesome way.

Playing flamenco allowed me to loosen up and be myself. If a passage or technique was too difficult, I had a license to change it within certain rules. Playing and performing were becoming workable for me in this medium.

One day, seemingly out of nowhere, my right wrist seized up. It was really painful for a few days, then is released. After a short time, it happened again. I talked to my teacher about it, who referred me to a physiotherapist who specialized in musicians' injuries. In our first appointment, she told me to cancel all my performances for the next year. I was only allowed to practice three 10-minute sets per day. I could increase the sets by a few minutes each week, as long as I was pain-free. I was so devastated that I didn't play for three weeks. It finally dawned on me that I'd never play again if I didn't start small. I was starting another long and painful process...

Fortunately, my yoga practice was alive and well. When my physio found out I did yoga, she said, "Never stop. If you do, your playing career will be over." This made perfect sense, as I'd previously uncovered that I had scoliosis, which was exacerbated by playing. With this new directive, though, I had a focus once again! Now, I did yoga and my physiotherapy exercises every day before I played my little sets. I also reworked my playing posture, my technique, my mindset, and even the way I breathed while playing.

I'm not going to lie; it was a brutal time. My body was my guru, telling me every moment when I was practicing properly and giving me stabbing pain when I wasn't. My income also suffered because I couldn't perform. I took some extra contracts teaching in schools. I was grateful for the work, but it wasn't what I loved. Still, I had a consistent income working about 25 hours per week. This allowed me the luxury of spending lots of time on my healing and retooling my playing, even though that didn't directly contribute to my bottom line in the short term.

In spite of my progress, I considered getting out of performing for good and just teaching. A voice rose up inside me, saying, "NO! If you don't figure out why this happened and heal it, you'll teach this debilitating way of playing to every one of your students." Disheartened as I was, I knew it was true. This hadn't been my first injury; I didn't know it then, but it wouldn't be my last, either. I knew I had to be patient and put one foot in front of the other, but it was excruciating.

After yoga had become an indispensable part of my practice regime, I decided to study it formally and get a certification. My guitar mentor was furious and insisted that I should focus on building my career as a musician. My response to my mentor was, "These things aren't separate. In India, musicians go into the temple and do yoga, meditate and play all day long. That's what I want." I heard the lightbulb go on.

My thought was that if I master yoga, I won't lose my career, but in case I do, I'll have another skill I love and am good at. A part of me secretly knew I had a second career brewing - and that by the time I got around to putting it out there as a business, I'd have a couple of decades of experience. I had no idea that the market was about to be saturated with yoga instructors and that I'd chosen a field with a worse money mindset than the arts and the non-profit sector combined.

In 2001, a week after 9/11, I started my 600-hour, 2-year Yoga teacher training program, the most comprehensive one in the country. The Yoga Centre of Calgary was the most respected studio in town at the time. That fall, the YCC lost four senior teachers to other studios; there were 11 new startups that opened in direct competition. One of the main ways they all generated base income was to offer teacher trainings - anywhere from 40 - 200 hours. The market was becoming saturated with competing studios and junior teachers who were encouraged to hang out their shingle the moment they stepped out of their training. Quality control became an industry-wide issue that's still unresolved today, and certification has become a business of its own.

It wasn't lost on me that the vast majority of "successful" yoga instructors I saw just happened to have husbands with well-paying jobs. There's no question that the work was deeply satisfying. But it seemed that burnout was a serious problem for most instructors who tried to create a profitable business.

In spite of that, I was hungry for knowledge, and I loved that part of my program included an in-depth mentorship with a senior teacher. Although the YCC folded at the end of my first year of training, I was still part of a well-connected network of teachers who'd come from a substantial yoga lineage. The instructor who handled our training classes came up with a plan right away to finish the program, almost exactly as it had been originally designed.

I never had any interest in owning a brick-and-mortar studio - the same was true for my guitar-teaching business; neither offered enough freedom for me. It made more sense to me to pay rent for the time I used only, so when I graduated, I started classes at a local community hall. They were somewhat successful, but it proved to be a lot of work to keep them full. As soon as I gave them up, the phone rang with guitar students who wanted those premium time spots for lessons - and the bottom line was more lucrative. After a few more laps around the track with studio-type situations, I gave up teaching yoga for a while… But in the meantime, another new topic had piqued my interest: Ayurveda!

Ayurveda is the naturopathic system that developed along with yoga in ancient India. It's based on three constitutional aspects; each person is their own unique mix. It has all manner of practitioners, from Ayurvedic doctors in India (whose training is on par with allopathic doctors here in the west) to those who teach Yoga from an Ayurvedic perspective, which was my plan.

I've got a pretty logical mind for an artist, and I found the blend of logic, intuition, and meditation to be a soulful way to learn. So I signed up for a 450-hour online course - again, with a mentorship component. I did the course with a friend, knowing that we'd work well together and hold each other accountable.

I'm really glad I did - knowing myself, I'm not sure I'd have finished otherwise.

It must have been my preoccupation with food for so many years that had me categorizing foods and lifestyle practices for each of the Ayurvedic types. When I finally focused on gut health with Big Gutsy Life, I found myself with a host of resources that I'd created without knowing exactly how I was going to apply them. Before I got there, though, I had to circle back on something that had been tugging at me for some time: Recording my album.

Year after year, every January 1st, recording my album was my only goal. In 2015, I got serious about it and started applying for grants. It turned out to be quite a process! Every time, I'd hear the feedback that my project was great, but funding was at an all-time low. I knew I needed to double down on my commitment to the project and that it was an inside job. I continued to take one step at a time toward my goal because I knew in my bones that it was going to happen.

In the end, I submitted eight applications to a total of 3 granting bodies. I took a significant personal risk in the process. I knew I wanted to workshop my compositions with a flamenco master in Spain. The overseas study that is so necessary for flamenco has several challenges. The first is that I had to be physically present to teach lessons. I arranged for my students to pay a monthly average so that I could take up to 4 weeks off throughout the teaching year. For this type of study, it's not a long time, but I've learned to make the most of it and wring out every bit of value I can - if my studio is full.

When I was making my travel plans for 2016, my studio *wasn't* full, not by any stretch. I had a 'come to Jesus' conversation with the universe (or, more accurately, with myself) that went something like this: "Look, I AM NOT booking my ticket to Spain until I know bills are going to be looked after. If You want me to do this, I need a full studio, dammit." Covering the dance classes seemed a little more challenging. The students weren't confident enough to hold their own without me. I needed a student player who could hold down the fort in my absence - not exactly something I could put into a job description.

With this vision in place, the phone started ringing. Within a few weeks, I had a schedule full of prepaid guitar students ready to start as soon as I returned. I also had a brand new keener who specifically wanted to mentor in dance accompaniment. He was ecstatic about my program and got up to speed in just a few lessons. It was like magic!!

The only hitch was that I didn't have funds for the trip. I'd applied for a grant but wouldn't know the outcome until after I returned. It was a bold move, but I decided to go anyway. If the grant didn't come through, there was my mortgage cash account. Yes, it WAS crazy, and I don't do that for just anything.

Here's the thing I've learned about being a rebel: I can't get away with anything. If I'm a Hell-Yes to something, I'm absolutely meant to do it. It's a mission that comes from so deep within me that I'm willing to crawl over glass to make it happen. That's not the same as telling the universe that I want a vacation, and I'm going to use my mortgage cash account unless the way is paved with gold stones. So I booked my ticket and went. In the end, I received the grant - which opened the door to receiving the recording grant, too. I received a second grant, which allowed my project to be very nicely funded. I'd be able to realize my vision for the recording.

In the meantime, I'd started working out at the gym, which I swore I'd never do in my life. I had all the rebel excuses for not going, but when I finally did, I loved it. For the first time, at the age of 47, I reclaimed every ounce of the energy I'd lost at 17 when I had mono and had to stop running track. Turned out it was necessary to do the recording project because I've never worked harder in my life. It took everything I had, and I'm glad I gave it all because I'm still enormously proud of the album - which went on to win three awards and received two more nominations.

If you didn't know the story, you might wonder how the two seemingly different paths of flamenco and gut health intersect. Yet there IS a relationship. In Ayurveda, the 'digestive fire' is known to be about so much more than the digestion of food. It's the power that digests life itself, sorting through all our experiences, emotions, impressions, and memories, keeping what nourishes us and discarding whatever is no longer of use. When it's functioning properly, it prevents whatever is wasteful or toxic in our experience from accumulating and clogging us up.

Much of the poor health I experienced in my teens, 20s, and even my 30s, was due to unmetabolized life experiences. My childhood was very stressful, I'd chosen difficult relationships, and I had a lot to deal with. Initially, playing music provided me with a way of coping and running the energy of my negative emotions through my system. Now, it's only one of many options at my disposal for accomplishing the same thing. And because my entire system is clearer in every way - emotionally and physically - it's also more efficient.

Today, I have no food sensitivities, no major injuries, and I feel emotionally well, but I still need to be aware. If I don't eat well, I can slip back into fatigue and brain fog. I need strong exercise to sleep well and to keep my body from returning to its old familiar scoliosis pattern. I've learned what I need, specifically, to take care of myself and keep my energy flowing well. If I don't, I end up feeling burnt out.

My method for helping others reach the same point has come from my own hard-earned knowledge, along with Ayurvedic wisdom for each of the types. When I first started consulting, I could scarcely believe how quickly my clients experienced results (I was almost jealous). It had taken me so long; I expected it to be a long and painful road for them, too. It's deeply gratifying to know that my journey is helping other people!

Here are some of the things I've learned:

- My business, my life, my terms. I have to do things my own way, even if it seems crazy sometimes.
- Mentorship plus being a Self-starter is my winning combination. Anytime I'm hungry for knowledge and deeply committed to my own growth, the next key piece shows up – in line with Divine Timing.
- Create consistent income using a business model that's bigger than hours for dollars.
- How we do one thing is how we do everything; the way you digest food is the way you digest life. I'm a powerhouse when I'm on my game and almost completely debilitated when I'm not - there isn't much middle ground.
- Don't compromise on balance, whatever that means for you. Know and honor yourself because YOU are the most important asset in your business.
- When it comes to sticky health issues, you need a team. I've never found all the answers from one source, but I have got some big pieces from solid professionals in their field. With some, I still call on their expertise after several decades.

When I look at my gut health method, it works as a holistic entrepreneurial model as well. See for yourself:

1. Re reset your nervous system. Just like you don't digest well in fight or flight, you can't run a business from there, either.
2. Discover and shift the subconscious beliefs that are keeping you (your body and your business) stuck.
3. Know your Gutsy Type, and which foods (impressions and experiences) are the right ones for you. Each Type also has certain personality traits that can either help you make headway or can hinder your progress. When you know what they are, you can become skilled in reaching for what's helpful and avoiding those personal traps that can be like kryptonite.
4. You learn how to get quiet, block out the noise, and listen to what your body and intuition are telling you.
5. We work out a plan for you to nourish your gut lining, increase the good gut bugs, and crowd out the bad ones. In business, nourish your foundation, surround yourself with the type of people who support you well.
6. Once your digestive system has been healed and reset, you can start expanding your list of "happy tummy" foods. Your business will also require you to expand when you'd rather contract.

There's no question I'm still learning; that's just how I'm wired. I always will be. All that time I spent on healing, studying, and self-development was like investing in stocks. I believe that investing in yourself always pays off. I've heard people say they can scarcely believe how much depth I have with so many things. Being well-paid for my billable hours has always put me in a position to develop; however, I've been called to do. For me, being multi-passionate is part of my balance. It's what keeps my work joyful!

Jacqueline St.Amand

Jacqueline, the owner of Gem Gallerie Jewellers, has been a Graduate Gemologist in the industry for over 20 years and has a deep love for creativity and gemstones. Her passion began when she discovered a stone called Benitoite from California and has been an avid Jeweller and gemologist for many years. Being fluently bilingual in both official languages has allowed her to work in the jewelry industry across Canada in both wholesale and retail environments. This diversity of experience and willingness to grow has given her a well-rounded knowledge of the jewelry industry. A knowledge that she willingly shares with colleagues and customers alike. Let her bring the sparkle back to your favorite jewelry.

Connect with Jacqueline:

https://gemgallery.com/

https://www.linkedin.com/in/jacqueline-st-amand-7553b420/

Chapter 6

Jewelry Heist Gone....Right!

By Jacqueline St. Amand

The long weekend was here at last. It had been months since I had taken any time off. Approaching the store, I realized something was off, so I went around back to disarm the alarm system. My remote access was still showing armed, so I thought maybe a leaky roof, which has happened throughout the complex before. I was greeted by a well-executed scene of destruction with glass and metal littering the floor. I paused and took the entire scene in, flabbergasted by the destruction. I called my husband, "Honey, are you at work yet.... Not yet ...could you come by the store? I need a hug!....I will be right there...Thanks, see you soon". A few numb moments passed. Then I started sweeping the largest of the glass debris and realized the time. Better call my employees and let them know what has happened. Afterward, I phoned the locksmith from my network groups, a couple of colleagues who had kindly left me goods on a memo, and the police. As the expression goes, I got blindsided on any given Tuesday. Of course, my mind and emotions bounced from one consideration/concern to another. Still, I focused on my mind's main points (action plan) and my emotion's underlying values (overall big picture goal) to avoid panic and find a way forward.

At some point during the days that followed, I heard a song from my past that chimed, "we're not gonna take it anymore… and we'll fight, you'll see." It so resonated with me; I decided at that moment I was not going to let this tragedy stop me, and I was not going to let others get burned because of this. From my 15-plus years in the industry, I knew bankruptcy would burn my suppliers and clients. Conservative estimates were around 2-3 months to open again. With the help of friends, family, and business networks, I re-opened in 3 weeks. It was critical, in my opinion, to re-open as soon as possible, as the faster we started operating again, the sooner the incoming cash flow could be used to take care of clients and suppliers whose items had been stolen. It was time to live up to my values from childhood and treat others the way I would like to be treated.

Precious Life Values

We didn't have much growing up, but my parents instilled a great work ethic in us kids, for which I am eternally grateful. If problems came along, of which there were many, we found a way to talk and work through them. Problems were like a puzzle or riddle that you just had to figure out a way to solve. It was always very clear that "money did not grow on trees," which was a great lesson to learn. I learned to make the most out of what I have and that you can live on less and still be happy (well, this came in handy after the robbery). Don't get me wrong: Mom and Dad would treat us when they could and would always fill the house with love. I still remember Mom saying, "appreciate what you have," and making sure we understood everything and everyone has value. I am proud to say no truer words were ever spoken, and I live it every day. Always make the most out of what you have, which leads to "waste not, want not," as Gramma used to say. I often thought of this during the cleanup and salvage; any little stone, charm, etc., gave me a little thrill in what appeared to be nothing but debris; there were finds that would help rebuild the store. Hour after hour, sweeping, sifting every pile through a filter before throwing it out.

"Never take anything or anyone for granted" was another saying from childhood that has stuck with me. Many opportunities in life will pass you by if you don't appreciate them at the time for the gift that they are and the people you meet. Those relationships are gold, and you need to feed those relationships with appreciation, as it is a form of respect. Think about the people in your life, how you treat them and how they treat you. It matters if either feels taken for granted or taken advantage of and will react by leaving that relationship. Without the relationships I had built over the years, I would never have been able to rebuild, and I know it, so I make sure all those helping hands and acts of kindness are expressly appreciated; I say it again. THANK YOU, one and all.

Another lesson from childhood that has served me well is if you want something, you have to work for it. I always feel a great sense of wonder and accomplishment after a job well done, a seemingly monumental goal achieved. Working for everything I ever needed or wanted so as not to be a burden on anyone around me has been a great way to grow confidence, resilience, and independence. Quite a change from the quiet, shy and introverted child of years gone by, being willing to try new things, whether it was food, drawing a picture, soccer, or writing this chapter. All these new experiences teach us something, help us grow, and sometimes even open new doors. My parents knew the best way for us kids to grow was to encourage us to try and keep learning, as education is a fabulous gift and tool to make your own path in life. Above all, treat others as we would like to be treated.

Treasured Experiences

From this very humble childhood, many life lessons came to form the foundation for the path my life's journey would take. Who would have thought I would eventually own and run my very own jewelry store? I certainly never did! I was a great student who loved to learn, whether hands-on, academic, or creative. So much, so the proud family joke was, I would be 80 and still taking courses.

So life's journey went on for many years and included many diverse interests and learning opportunities: Art, Psychology, electronic assembly, French, soccer. Upon completing my first college degree in social science with the intent of entering the Psychology field to help people, fate intervened, and I heard a conversation two grad students had about how they did not know what to do next. They had graduated but needed to get into the Masters' program in order to practice psychology, but there was a five-year waiting list and required a 95% average and above to even be considered! Well, was I glad I heard that conversation because my current 85% average just would not cut it, and university tuition was steep. It was time to pick a new direction.

I continued working in the electronic assembly that had paid for my schooling thus far until I figured out what next. Fast forward a year, and I had my answer. I was riding the bus to work like I always did, and I overheard two guys talking about this really cool stone with a steely blue color that shined like a diamond but was only found on 10 square acres in San Benito County, California. Sitting there completely enraptured, listening in on their conversation, I had an Aha moment! I told myself if it interested me enough to be rude and listen in on someone's conversation, there was definitely something there!

Time for another degree, but this time it was Jewelry Arts, a vocational 3-year college program only available at the French college, as I could not find a Gemology program. Thankfully I had the beautiful gift of being bilingual (languages are beautiful tools, the more of them you know, the more versatile you can be). I figured jewelry and gems go hand in hand, so I would eventually find a gemology program, which was what I was really after. I did well in the first term but was so enthralled with the jewelry fabrication process that I signed up for the private gemology program as well and completed both programs! The rest is history, so they say. I have been in the jewelry industry for over 20 years now, and I am still learning and loving it. It took a lot of hard work and long hours doing full-time schooling and working at the same time to pay for it. But it was all worth it! My gemology teacher and first true mentor saw something within and offered me the first-ever scholarship towards the first class of the professional GIA Graduate Gemologist program. I was flabbergasted! This was life-changing; the program was expensive and out of reach, but I told myself if she believed in me that much, I don't know how, but I had to find a way. More hard work, accumulating enough cash to pay for the next class, which I flew through with flying colors in record time, more work and saving for the next class was how the cycle went until I eventually completed my GIA Graduate Gemologist diploma, which is an internationally known and recognized accreditation.

I did not even know what networking was at the time. I just always liked to greet people, learn about them, and always wanted to lend a helping hand. Apparently, I had been networking since school; I just didn't know it, and it opened many doors. The key here, though, is you have to recognize that it is a door opening and take a chance, do something that scares you a little and walk through that door because who knows where it will lead you. This little girl from a poor background and no family history of entrepreneurship or jewelry background whatsoever, by society's standards, would definitely be an underdog for becoming a Graduate Gemologist/Appraiser, silversmith, and jewelry store owner, but here I am. Your background does not have to hold you back. Mine didn't. I chose to work at what I wanted to achieve next, like stepping stones, learning through the journey, and becoming more resilient and confident along the way. Before I knew it, I was being asked by friends and family why I didn't own my own store. "You know and have worked in many aspects of the jewelry industry, have led officially and unofficially for years," to which my typical responses would be, "Nah, I love what I do too much. Besides, I don't have enough experience for that" or "Thanks, of course, you would say that because you're supposed to be my cheerleader."

Cherished Events

Then life gave me a unique learning opportunity. The goldsmith at the store I was working at wanted to start his own store and needed/wanted me to come work for him to set it up and take care of customers. I talked it over with my husband; this was a very risky proposition, giving up a well-paying job to go to a startup. I did not candy coat it; I wanted to do this for the chance to see how a startup jewelry store journey begins and what it entailed, knowing full well many new startups fail. But, at least, I would be able to see what it was all about and if I wanted that for myself or not.

It was a unique opportunity being able to help be part of a new startup without any capital investment. As I expected, being the only non-family member on the team when things started out too slow (it takes three years on average for a new jewelry store to build up clientele enough to make a profit) and money was running out, I was let go. It was ok, though, as I gained a wealth of knowledge, and leaving freed up the capital they needed to survive. I am happy to say they are still in operation; we still collaborate and refer clients back and forth. This experience also gave me a valuable golden nugget of information. If I was ever going to own a store, I definitely did not want to do a new startup.

After many months of looking for new work, I was frequently being told I was over-qualified or not the right fit for the company: "Need employees that look pretty and hard sell only…or …we need closers for today's sale, never mind tomorrow ...or… what the client wants or needs is not important, we need to sell X # of this product this month". Wow, what an attitude to have with those who trust you with their hard-earned money to celebrate one of life's important moments! Then I found the Gem Gallerie, thanks to my industry network of colleagues, a lovely local, comfortable, and chic family-run jewelry store that has been around since the early 80s. I swung by at the owner's request for an informal meet and interview. We hit it off right away, though there was no current official job opening. We both came to the conclusion that I would be a good fit. Having worked in a few toxic environments in the past, realizing that this was a big step for the Gallerie as they have had a few toxic employees in the past, I offered to work pro bono/volunteer for one month so we could both try each other out. If nothing else, it would help grow my network and keep me busy for a while rather than sitting around trying to find another job.

It worked out fabulously. They were the perfect match with great people that have stayed with the company for 25 years through thick and thin and welcomed me with open arms and gratitude for the extra help and expertise that I brought to the table. We all mutually agreed that I would stay on full-time and ease some pressure off of everyone. My new colleagues were happy for some experienced help and soon became my biggest cheerleaders with our regular clients so the clients would be more comfortable with a new face at the store. As time wore on, I started helping with some of the management tasks, and the owner asked me to join her for her networking breakfast, as she wanted me to get networking and known as an expert at the store. This was when I realized I was an appreciated expert at the Gem Gallerie, and I had been networking all along as a connector in a small way my whole career. Little did I know the owner was slowly grooming me to be the new face of the Gem Gallerie, and I would be taking over more and more tasks. To my surprise, my colleagues were happy about it and relieved that it was not falling to them. They have been with the company almost since the beginning and have been overworked for years. They really needed a break, and now they could have it.

Fast forward a couple of years during a 1-2-1 with a new member of our networking group; within 15 minutes, he asked me, "So why don't you have your own store???" The same question family and friends have asked me for years (of course, I share those stories with him), this time coming from a complete stranger! Well, this caused me to pause as he asked a few more pointed questions. I realized he had a point and also that he had wisdom that did not come from his current career hat. So I called him on it: "These are very insightful questions not common to your current field of expertise. What did you do before this?" A nanosecond of a pause: "You're right. A very astute observation, by the way. I used to be a business coach." Well, that explained the questions, but now I really had to listen to what life has been trying to tell me all along: I should be open to owning my own store. His last statement, "What is stopping you, money?? That is easy and can work itself out." Of course, my curious perpetual learner of a mind had a burning question; what did he see that made him think I could or should run my own business? You are passionate, knowledgeable, has integrity, and have a great drive to get things done. This was definitely another life-changing moment; another door was about to open. I just had to be ready to turn the handle and walkthrough.

The Silver Lining

A sudden death in the family caused a shift for us all. Having worked for a family-run business my entire career, I have seen them close, and what that shutdown did to the communities they were in. It's like a small piece of the community died. I had a gut feeling from the way the owner was acting that she was going to shut it down. With the responsibility of the multiple businesses her husband was running now on her shoulders, it was too much. This was the door, but did I finally have enough courage to do something that scares me a little…Absolutely! I love this gem of a store, its clients, and my colleagues too much to watch it close. I reached out to my business network, the accountant first and the corporate lawyer second, to figure out the details and how risky it would be. It turned out my plan was a good one. The next step was to ask my colleagues if they would stay on if I bought the store. This was a vital part of the plan, as they have been the face of the store for years; they had the trust of the clients, so I would definitely need them to make the transition easier. I realized without them; this would not work. They said, "For you, yes. For anyone else, no!" Wow, I was flattered and relieved by their confidence! The last step was to ask the current owner if she would sell. Without hesitation, she said, "Yes, I was hoping you would ask; you already take good care of our store, and I really don't want to watch it close, but I have too much to handle right now." The rest is now history.

The heist mentioned at the beginning of this chapter occurred within the first year of owning the store, which is definitely a huge obstacle to overcome for a green entrepreneur like myself. Little did I know that my immediate action to take care of my customers and re-open quickly would fast-track my credibility in the community. In a way, the most devastating loss of my inventory became an opportunity to show my network, my community, and my colleagues how devoted I am to doing the right thing; that resilience is possible in the face of adversity, and how it gave me an opportunity to refresh the inventory and re-merchandise the store. Networking is a huge key to a successful business, as many of us are experts in our field but not an expert in all fields. That is where networking comes in. By meeting and forming relationships with diverse individuals, you can find the experts you need to help your business grow. Maybe you need an accountant, a lawyer, or a marketing specialist but can't pay one full time. Look in your network, and you will probably find one that will take you on as a client. Those same contacts can become great referral partners if you build the relationships.

Stability also helps create confidence in your company in the face of adversity. Had I waited too long to re-open, many would have wondered if I was ever going to re-open, and client confidence would have plummeted. When COVID came along, I learned that stability went a long way to building client trust. When the world was reducing its hours, going by appointment only, reducing its advertising, I saw unease set in and a lot of talk in the media about businesses going bankrupt. People needed a sense of stability; they needed to see you putting in the effort to move forward, especially in difficult times. Stability is like emotional comfort food; when it is there, you feel more comfortable that everything will work out in the end. Though it was hard, I kept my regular hours of operation and stayed visible both in my networks and in advertising. Besides the old adage "be seen or be forgotten," there was no way I was leaving my slowly rebuilding business unattended and closed. That would have been an open invitation to get broken into all over again. Paranoid? Maybe a little, but that is ok because that was one risk I was not willing to take! Taking a chance on owning a business, pivoting my life path, learning new things, trying new things, and being open to talk about all that has transpired is all worth taking a chance to pursue.

Karen Bodoano

The unstoppable Karen Bodoano credits her thirty years of management at Sentinel Self-Storage as the inspiration behind becoming the founder and CEO of Alberta's Move Coordinators, a business built on transforming the stressful complexities of home relocation into an easy, efficient one-stop-shop experience.

Karen always had an affinity for the elderly, noticing that, in the absence of family, they would end up mistreated, even cheated by scurrilous, low-rate moving companies. Ultimately stepping up herself as an advocate, she became a trained professional organizer and Western Canada's first certified senior move manager.

The determined go-getter set about facilitating every aspect of the process for older adults, even masterminding www.*NewlyMine.com*, an online auction to effectively sell their downsized belongings. Only the second Edmontonian to join NASMM, her profession's national association, Karen is a speaker and workshop leader at their annual conferences. She is a proud contributor to this literary compilation, reminding us that optimizing adversity is about perseverance and unwavering faith. Never give up on your dreams!

Connect with Karen:

https://www.linkedin.com/in/karen-bodoano-0b9a041/

https://www.movecoordinators.ca/

info@movecoordinators.ca

https://www.facebook.com/karen.bodoano

Chapter 7

Can't Take The Saskatchewan Out of The Kid

By Karen Bodoano

Growing up on a farm in northwest Saskatchewan in the seventies was idyllic. It was rare to have the whine of a siren pierced the air. Neighbors looked out for each other and lent a hand.

Most lived on mixed family farms, making enough to earn a living but not enough to grow prosperous. We didn't feel the sting of not having as much as other kids. Designer clothes and fancy cars weren't part of the landscape of anyone we knew. Most of us wore hand-me-downs, with the occasional new outfit from the Sears catalog or local SAAN store. We attended school with the same students, year after year. Our small class sizes meant teachers could provide ample attention. They noticed if anyone dared to skip a class, let alone a day! An absence guaranteed a call home, so skipping was rare. There was nothing to do, anyway. As there were no malls to hang out in, the local shoppers at the Co-op would be certain to question why we weren't at school. By graduation, my classmates felt like brothers and sisters.

I was the kid that enjoyed every part of the school. The oldest of four, it was where I could go to escape my home life. In five years, my mom had given birth to three more children. I was seven when my youngest sister was born. Mom was tired, worn out, and much too thin. Black circles around her eyes made her eye sockets appear hollow. When I overheard hushed voices speak about Mom having "bad nerves," I imagined a network of vessels under her skin that just didn't work.

I was too young to know that not all moms walked the floor and talked to themselves. Like a pent-up zoo animal, she paced. I watched her laugh and argue with the voices in her head or lie on her bed and stare at the ceiling. During this period, Dad was working long hours on the farm. Covered with grime, he would return to the farmhouse at suppertime. As the oldest, I knew instinctively I must watch over my three preschool siblings. We escaped outdoors and explored every nook and cranny of the farm.

In the summer of 1971, Mom reached a breaking point. Mom and us four children were shuttled to my grandmother's home in Edmonton while Mom was under a doctor's care. Grandma was strict. She came home from work, cooked, bathed all four of us, and had us in bed at 7:00 pm. I recall laying in crisp linens as the curtains swayed in the breeze. It was hard to grasp why I couldn't be outside playing with other seven-year-olds. My blonde, blue-eyed, rambunctious little brothers, at four and two-and-a-half, itched for freedom! As farm kids, we didn't understand the concept of being locked inside a fenced yard. We longed for our farm home and Dad.

We returned to the farm for school in the fall. Unfortunately, Mom's illness was not over. She was hospitalized in the North Battleford mental hospital with a nervous breakdown. My aunt and uncle, who lived north of Goodsoil, took us four little kids in. They had raised seven kids of their own and now had four more, ranging from 10 months to seven years. More than ever, the school was my escape.

Just before Christmas, Mom came home, subdued and heavily medicated. She slept a lot but did keep up with house cleaning, laundry, and meals. Expected to pitch in more and more, I cherished my time at school and worked as hard as I could to earn my teachers' praise.

After a few years of elementary school, I noticed other moms were different. Visits to my friends' homes revealed a completely different atmosphere. Initially, I discounted this, thinking their mothers must not have "bad nerves" inside of them.

Our situation led Dad to work harder than ever on the farm. He added more cattle and more land. Dad had grown up with six strong, independent sisters and a pioneer mother—all capable of working as hard as any man on a farm. His wife was petrified of driving. When it came time to shuttle vehicles from field to field, Mom froze with fear behind the wheel. She tired easily and couldn't tolerate any physical labor. Even gardening was too taxing.

Frustrated by Mom's weakness, he pushed me to take over when Mom was unwell. Clean, cook, garden—these became my day-to-day activities. He yelled when I wasn't able to drive as well as he wanted, scaring me to freeze like Mom. It was a relief my little brother Kevin loved everything related to operating machinery. He jumped in at age seven!

Dad also insisted we all do better in school. He was especially tough on me as the oldest. A's weren't enough—why not Apluses? I rushed to show him my reports cards, excited to show off the marks I had worked so hard to achieve, only to have him focus on the one lowest score. It created a vicious trait of perfectionism.

Now, almost 50 years later, I'm thankful he insisted I tackle farm jobs. Women's lib was a new catchphrase in the sixties and seventies, but farm families lived it well before it was socially accepted. If you had two hands and a strong body, gender did not matter. He taught me many basic lessons about agriculture, animal husbandry, carpentry, and mechanics.

Dad was an active volunteer in the community and served in many capacities, but the difficulties at home led him to favor alcohol. As my teenage years arrived, he withdrew from everyone and spent more time searching for answers at the bottom of a bottle. This dad was angry and bitter. I kept my distance.

In 1981, I graduated at the top of my class and was chosen as valedictorian. Reading my speech today, I marvel at the cliches I wrote about the role of adulthood. Under the flowery phrases was a teen that wanted to go to university or college. Unbeknownst to me, Dad was under extreme financial pressure operating the family farm during a time of crippling interest rates. He had gambled and taken on too much debt. Dad never worried us, kids, about the details, but the stress weighed heavily on him. Three kids at home still needed raising, and money for postsecondary just wasn't there. Life forced me to pivot—change course, and adjust my sails.

I would need to move to get work. Edmonton, Saskatoon, and Lloydminster were all possibilities. Dad gave me $100 when I told him I was moving to Edmonton to live with my cousin's girlfriend. He was perturbed that I would commit to an apartment lease before I had a job.

My cousin Les fronted my share of the first month and my half of the damage deposit. "You're just going to party in the city for a month or two, then you'll be home," he predicted.

I vowed to myself I would succeed if only to prove him wrong. Once in Edmonton, with a couple of boxes of pots, pans, and other household items, I settled into a two-bedroom apartment. It was located right next door to an ambulance station. Every time I dozed off, sirens screamed and I jumped awake.

I remember watching the CN tower's neon light through my bare bedroom window. It chased its way around the racetrack—C, then N—then start again. "Wow," I thought. "This is the big time."

Eager to get started on my new life, I bought the Edmonton Journal daily and applied for every job in sight. Within ten days, I was working at Amalgamated Credit Union, within walking distance from our bare-bones apartment. I was proud to land a job as a teller. The monthly wage was $750 per month gross, $600 net. My rent was 180 dollars. After utilities and groceries, there wasn't much left, but I paid Les back the 360 dollars I owed him. I had no furniture and slept on foam on the floor. My open suitcases served as dresser drawers. After a few months, I signed a 400-dollar loan and bought myself a bedroom suite. Each month, I paid 50 dollars toward my debt. I was so proud to manage my own affairs.

In the summer, I walked ten blocks to work, tromping down 105 Street in high-heeled shoes. I didn't realize that route was frequented by working girls. Following more than one screaming confrontation, I adjusted my route and stopped wearing high heels to avoid being mistaken for a call girl.

I was surprised to find my work fulfilling and enjoyable. That was fortunate because returning home, where there were no jobs, was not an option. My family's difficulties had grown worse. Lenders repossessed four of the five quarters of land and the farming equipment. They negotiated the debt in a way that allowed the family to stay on the quarter of land with our home and farmyard. Dad left for weeks on end to work, leaving my two youngest siblings at home with still-fragile Mom. The alcoholism raged, and their financial situation was precarious.

Stress led Mom to stop taking her medication. A roller coaster of manic, hostile behavior followed, then hospitalization. I made repeated trips home to try to negotiate with the madness and get her to come to the hospital with me. Sometimes I lied to get her in the vehicle. At eighteen, a kind mental health nurse told me that this behavior was part of Mom's illness—paranoid schizophrenia. It's a moment that is forever locked in my memory. The words hit me like a locomotive careening down a mountain. The adults in my life had sugar-coated the truth to protect us. There were no "bad nerves" or "nervous breakdowns." Mom had a lifelong disease that impacted all of us. In the early years, doctors treated her chemical imbalance with shock therapy. Now, she has been prescribed a cocktail of medication.

At that time, mental illness was not something anyone spoke about. As an adult, I came to suspect Mom may have suffered from postpartum depression after the birth of Shelly.

I began to read as much as I could. My siblings and I questioned her caregivers. Dad maintained a denial of her diagnosis. He often stated his belief that she was trying to get attention, and it was all a show. For many years, the stigma was too great for him to acknowledge and accept.

I met my first husband in the fall of 1981. Hurt and worry flashed over Dad's face when we started living together and soon after became engaged. At nineteen, I was certain this was the path for me.

Banking suited me. I like the exactness, structure, and process. The management was patient, but expectations were high. It was the perfect starting point for a small-town kid. As opportunities arose, I enrolled in evening accounting classes. Dad had always said education was key to success. I agreed with him—no one could ever take it away from you. Just as in my childhood, education was a refuge.

I made many friends at the Credit Union but grew restless. After seven years of rushing up the administration side of the ladder, I was no longer learning enough to keep me interested. I had mastered my day-to-day tasks and longed for new challenges. While my efforts were recognized in the beginning with a series of quick promotions, I had stalled. My goal was to advance into lending, but every application was turned down, leaving me frustrated by the "glass ceiling" so many women in banking faced in the early eighties.

My best friend, Lucille, challenged me. She suggested I make one last attempt to obtain a job in lending. If passed over again, I must decide to either find work elsewhere or accept it and stop complaining.

I began taking accounting courses and set myself the goal of finding a small office where I could get some experience in a variety of accounting aspects, from accounts receivable to payroll. I targeted small business accounting roles. Sentinel's ad was small and obscure. My insides were fluttering when I arrived for the interview. Bruce, the controller, needed an office manager. The job offered all the experience I hoped to gain in my career path.

A few days later, Bruce called with the news. I'd lost to a candidate already familiar with their computer program "Framework," but I was their second choice. Trying to hide my disappointment, I wished him well. A book I had embraced, *What Color is Your Parachute,* recommended sending a handwritten thank you card following job interviews. I dashed off a quick note and dropped it in the mail, never expecting a response, and went on to accept a job doing collections on outstanding mortgage payments for a now-defunct Alberta government program. A few weeks later, Bruce called. Their first candidate hadn't worked out. Was I still interested?" My husband and I debated the risk of leaving the security of my government job to work for a small start-up company. I was already certain that I was not a good fit with the government.

I was 24 when I walked into Sentinel's second-floor offices. It was soon obvious—the job was everything I'd hoped. Not one day was routine or boring. Whenever I approached the owner to discuss a challenge, he posed thoughtful questions to help me analyze the situation and reach the solution myself. Bill valued technology and constantly pushed staff to find tools to help us be more productive and stay relevant. Perhaps best of all, he encouraged me to further my education and invested Sentinel dollars into my education! A leader and mentor, rather than just a manager, he taught me how to help staff be the best they could be. I evolved into someone I would not have predicted 29 years earlier. At the age of 26, I became the operations manager, overseeing about 20 employees. When I left in September 2017, the company had grown from four to twenty-five locations across Canada.

During my time at Sentinel, my husband and I decided we were ready to become parents. After several years without success, we sought medical assistance. In the nineties, however, there were fewer infertility solutions. We struggled through tests and procedures. Each month brought another disappointment. The failure drove a wedge into our relationship. Adoption options were limited, with wait times approaching ten years. Typical for those with our stoic farm upbringings, we swallowed our pain and carried on. In retrospect, we should have sought counseling. As the time ticked away, it became apparent to us that our ages—Kevin, 40, and me, 35—made us too old to become parents.

I threw myself into work and being an auntie. For the second time, I was forced to pivot away from a vital desire and change course. I adjusted my sails into new winds, with the education my familiar refuge. It was exciting to return to my long-held desire to go to university and take advantage of offerings from the University of Alberta Continuing Education department. With Bill's encouragement, I signed up for Toastmasters and honed my public speaking skills. This pivot led me to become a more competent leader at Sentinel.

By 2015, my marriage was faltering. Perfectionists hate to fail, but something needed to change. We entered counseling; unfortunately, the chasm between us was great. No one prepares you for the fact that you and your partner change. With great sadness and a shroud of fear, I moved out. My coping mechanism was to throw myself into work; however, more change was in the wind. A large storage company in Ontario had gone public, and Sentinel was a prized portfolio. It was sold in

July 2017 for 396 million dollars. My intention was to stay. I liked the industry and, most of all, the people. We had dedicated staff, and our many long-term employees formed a family-like culture. I was offered vice-president Operations of Alberta, which involved overseeing 30 locations.

The new company set its tone quickly. The focus was short-term, always the bottom line. This was at the cost of every area Sentinel prided itself on—caring for staff, customers, and property. Our Cadillac portfolio, highly valued and sought after by several large national companies, was now being stripped down, cannibalized, and "Wal-martized" to satisfy a competitive market.

Unlike the leadership model I was accustomed to, the new management ran operations with little thought or regard to the impact on staff. They enjoyed wielding their power and belittling staff. I observed my new colleagues bully and demand. Stomp on and correct. There were no kind words of encouragement, mentorship, or pride in work well done. Always, there was the constant undertone of "you can be replaced." My working environment departed from the class and grace I had known to one of suspicion and contempt. Where was I? Everything in me knew there was no way I could participate in this nasty behavior.

So, now what? After observing yet another staff member being berated for petty infractions by a contemporary, my heart sunk. My colleague watched my face for a reaction, hoping I was on board with her approach. "This is how we do it here," gleaned from her agitated eyes.

The harsh reality hit me. The Sentinel I knew, loved, and grown with was gone. I could not be the change agent the new owners wanted. Nor was it possible for me to lead the charge to tear down what Sentinel had so carefully built. Bill understood the correlation of give and take; expect results but also reward excellence. Staff was valued stakeholders, not disposable commodities.

My solution was to leave. It was a difficult decision to close the door on a 29-year career that provided growth, achievements, and friendships. It was time to leave the security blanket of salary, benefits, and rank.

I took some time to heal and think. Good fortune brought a new partner into my life which much love and support.

My time at Sentinel had taught me that moving was one of the most stressful times of life. I often observed people, especially seniors, trying to navigate their moves. Many were enticed to hire the least costly movers, and the unregulated moving industry left them vulnerable to scam artists.

I realized I could make a difference by becoming what I thought of like a wedding planner for moving. But was there such a thing? My heart skipped a beat when during a Google search, I discovered an entire industry devoted to senior move management. I had found my clan! A surge of exhilaration flowed through my fingers as I typed my membership application for the National Association of Senior Move Management (NASMM).

With plenty of pivoting experience behind me, I repeated what had always worked. I signed up for courses. Educating myself in a new yet similar industry was invigorating!

In February 2018, I attended my first NASMM conference and experienced the power of being surrounded by 500 people—mostly strong, independent women—with similar goals. I held back tears of joy and relief as each person I met glowed with enthusiasm for the work they did. Enveloped in open arms, the clan elders made room for one more. This overjoyed apprentice took a seat and absorbed their advice and stories.

The conference throbbed with noticeable energy. Attendees buzzed and radiated positive beams about their meaningful work. It reminded me so much of the early days in the storage business when the people around me cared about meeting customer needs rather than the bottom line.

I discovered many companies had been in business for five to 15 years. Some had teams of 20 or more staff. Several had franchised. Others branched into other cities. I learned that not only was the work rewarding and necessary, but it was also possible to make a living at it. I came away inspired and encouraged.

Since then, it has been my goal to attend as many NASMM conferences as possible. It was a great honor to present a five-minute Ignite presentation in San Diego in 2019. I was fortunate to be selected to facilitate a workshop for my contemporaries in March 2020, just days before the world was stopped by COVID.

The course work was interesting and relatable. In 2019, I proudly became the first in Western Canada to earn the Certified Senior Move Manager designation.

To add to my credentials, I joined the local Professional Organizers of Canada (POC). What a wonderful sisterhood this is, as well as a source of more education! Our local POC chapter is made up of strong, capable women. It gives me great pride to be part of this dynamic group. Now that I am established, I can return the favor and deliver mentoring of my own.

Having my own company is the hardest thing I have ever done. The hours are long. Each day I wake up with the realization that my fledgling business relies entirely on my own actions to survive. I may not have enjoyed motherhood, but some days Move Coordinators is like a colicky infant—impossible to appease. There has been blood, sweat, tears, angst, and sleepless nights. The investment of money, energy, and time is more than I could have anticipated.

This has also been the most rewarding period of my career. It is not easy to reinvent yourself at 54. Becoming accustomed to a steady paycheque landing in your bank account without delay twice a month is great. But, nothing is sweeter than earning the funds that flow into your company bank account. The realization that every penny produced arises from your own efforts, ideas, and vision are wonderful. Watching Move Coordinators grow into a bonafide presence in the Edmonton market is immensely rewarding.

Like my clients' children, I am also trying to assist my senior parents with their aging journey. This humbling experience helps me honor and assist my clients.

All of my experiences have shaped me into the entrepreneur I am today. I credit my mentors-— the strong women who have served as role models, as well as my family and, most of all— my mother. At 81, she continues to persevere under difficult circumstances. She has shown me stereotypes do not exist, and uniqueness must be embraced and celebrated. It's a lesson I apply to my senior clients, as well as to my personal life.

I've expanded my ability to pivot when the winds change and find new paths. When life throws a Plan B, I know how to pivot, adjust my sails, and find joy in the new path. Although I was not able to raise children, I did have more time to develop my career and spend time with extended family and friends. Though leaving Sentinel was disappointing, it was also a change that allowed me to pursue a career I could never have anticipated. As Dad insisted, never stop learning. Toastmasters enabled me to become a trainer and accept speaking engagements. My University of Alberta courses built the skills I needed at Sentinel and— even more so—as the owner of my own company. My memberships in professional associations have enriched my life. My curiosity and quest for knowledge, inspired by Dad, have served me well. There is a joke that you can take the farm kid out of Saskatchewan, but you will never take Saskatchewan out of the farm kid. I know more adventures are ahead and am grateful for my upbringing and my ability to overcome challenges as I continue forward in everchanging winds.

Karla Weiss

Karla has led an impressive career over the years as a Registered Nurse, along with being an Amen Clinic Brain Health Coach and Holistic Health Coach. In 2021, she co-authored her amazing story in the compilation book, "Women Like Me - Volume 3," She is a passionate speaker who has had many opportunities to share the importance of having a healthy body, renewed mind, and restored soul so that one can achieve wholeness in all areas of their lives.

Karla is the CEO/Founder of Radically Transformed Coaching, where she has served women with a passion to develop a renewed and fresh outlook for their health. Through her Program, "Your Brain Counts," she helps people develop a specific roadmap to gain mastery over their sleep so they can feel and be their best in all that they do.

Karla is married to her husband of over 23 years and a busy mother to four children. For fun, she loves to scrapbook, walk outdoors, go camping and read.

Connect with Karla:

www.yourbraincounts.com

karla@yourbraincounts.com

Chapter 8

Watch Me Stumble Through Stuttering

By Karla Weiss

As far back as I can remember, I stuttered. I knew the words I wanted to say, but I couldn't get them out. The one thing that did come out was awkward sounds that had no meaning at all. I would try so hard to speak, but my words were all so broken up. It was humiliating and embarrassing. It is my intention through my story to share with others, being on 100 stages to speak to others, inspiring others to persevere in their pain and brokenness.

I used to be a bubbly, energetic child, but the more I became aware of my stuttering, my voice became silenced. I didn't want to say anything for fear it wouldn't come out right because of the stuttering. From an early age, I quickly became aware of what I was – a stutterer. Looking back, this "label" would carry with me for a long time.

School was the hardest to face. I didn't want to be different. I want to be like the others. I wanted to fit in. Talk normally and not get teased or laughed at. It got to a point where I would obsessively practice my words just so I could be more confident in my speech. I was tired of teasing, and I wanted to prove to my peers that I was just like them. When I learned to relax with my speech, I noticed the stuttering slowly disappeared. However, whenever I got nervous, excited, or upset, the stuttering showed its ugly face again. It just took time, lots of perseverance, determination, and putting one foot in front of each other day after day. My mother was a huge encouragement to me, giving me the strength I needed to keep going. I remember many times before I would dial the number of who I wanted to call, I would repeatedly practice the sounds and words I was having trouble saying.

BUT I persevered.

I was determined to overcome this impediment. Each time I tried proceeding with saying a word that I knew I would struggle with, I would practice it before attempting to say it in front of someone. I cried and wept many times because I literally hated myself for being so different. Why did God inflict me with this? WHY couldn't I be like the other kids? My self-confidence, body image, and self-concept were so low at this time.

As I wrote this story, I remember that I was different, and I couldn't stop thinking this way. I was a shy, insecure blonde little girl, and this shyness, this insecurity, and, of course, the stuttering grew more and more as I got older. I hid behind my mom wherever we went. I always found security with my parents, and I felt too afraid to be with other kids my age. It wasn't until I was in junior high that I really tried fitting in.

My insecurity was hidden at school by not wanting to answer any questions in class or avoiding interactions with others. The worst was when I tried to avoid at all costs doing any type of class presentations or projects that would put me in front of anyone, especially my own classmates. I didn't want to be humiliated because I couldn't get out my words. So, I remained silent and unnoticed as best as I could. Food became my source of comfort, but this only led to gaining weight, which only made things worst. Now I was the chubby, insecure, stuttering idiot at school.

This only pushed me further into a deep dark hole of sadness, depression, self-pity, and poor self-image. I tried fitting in wherever I went, but I was just so insecure; it was crippling. I had such negative self-talk about myself. I would look into the mirror sometimes and only see "a fat kid" or "an ugly kid."

The farm was my refuge, and I loved riding my bike everywhere just by myself on our long driveway and the many country roads that were around us. I would bike for miles and think, dream or even imagine what my life would be like when I got older or if I would ever stop stuttering. Would anyone want to marry me when I got older? Would I have kids? Why did I feel so different from the other kids?

Oh, I loved to ride my bike, for miles, on the country roads and even to the city. I would ride to the highest points either on the country road or over our property at the back end of the fields and watch the landscape or even the many colors from the sunsets or sunrises. Often on a clear day, we could see the tips of the mountains in the distance. God certainly has a way of painting beautiful tapestries and beautiful scenes in nature. Oh, let me not forget the stars in the sky, sparkling so brightly. Being on the farm and away from the city, it got pretty dark, like pitch dark; you couldn't even see anything. But those stars, the moon, and the Northern Lights shined so brightly. Even at times, we would be able to experience the Northern Lights dancing across the sky. Incredible!

As I biked, I enjoyed seeing the beautiful flowers that grew in the ditches to tasting the glorious saskatoons that grew wild on the edges of the fields. I would lay down on the ground and imagine what it would be like to fly free like a bird or how far heaven was from the earth where no one could find me and wondered what it was like. No one could see or hear my hurt. I wanted to soar like an eagle over mountain tops and leave the ache and emptiness I was feeling. I could sit out on the patio at night and gaze at the bright stars. I remember hearing the coyotes howling at night all around us, and our two German Shepherds would give them a howl back. All in all, I could escape my thoughts, feelings, and anything else bringing me down. It was my way of feeling that I wasn't being judged or laughed at. I am so glad that I had the experience of farm life.

A couple of years later, during grade 9, while enjoying life as usual on the farm, a tragedy occurred. It was spring and time to seed the ground. The time where it is filled with long days, late nights, and early mornings. All else was put on hold to get the work done no matter the cost. This one day, while out with my brothers, enjoying the smells, sounds, and activities on the farm, my parents had already left to head to the city. The cultivator had to be looked at before being ready to do its job. The wings of the cultivator were chained up as the hydraulic lines had been disconnected. I was alongside my one brother, helping to get things ready and hook up these hydraulic lines. We were getting all checks completed so all could run smoothly before heading out to the field. My other brother was doing the final checks and making sure it all was completed but made a tragic mistake.

The one brother that I was beside was situated close to a wheel, holding a pipe wrench in his hands. My other brother was on the opposite side of the cultivator. For whatever reason, he chose to undo those chains that held up the cultivator wings, and they came crashing down to the ground. That pipe wrench saved my brother's leg as it broke in half. I saw this contraption falling, and with all that I had, all the fight and flight power I had inside of me, I attempted to hightail out of there but was caught by the razor-sharp blades used to dig up the land. Those blades caught me in the front part of my forehead, an inch away from my right eye, and nicked me in the back of my head. With this massive blow to my head, I was thrown to the ground.

I wasn't sure how much time passed or if I was knocked out unconsciously, but I was able to get up. I quickly ran to the house and looked in the bathroom mirror; I became aware of the extent of my injury. I'm surprised I didn't pass out as blood gushed down my face. Wow. This was not just a small cut but a major alteration to my forehead. My brothers chased after me to the house to make sure I was ok. My eldest brother asked me to tell him how many fingers he was holding up. I was fine but didn't let him know. I answered with the wrong answer each time he asked me. I could just see his face get whiter and whiter and the panic in his face. Off to the hospital, we went.

We passed our parents on the highway, who quickly turned around and met us at the hospital to take over. My eldest brother was sent back home once we arrived to make sure my other brother was ok. Not great timing with all of this, as this was the week of the Choir Festival at school, and I was left with a huge bandage on my forehead. Oh great, not only was I struggling with stuttering, fitting in, being teased for being different than everyone else, but I now had a disfiguration on my forehead, and this big brown bandage really made me stand out everywhere. To make matters worse, I was also in the front row for the festival...This was not my shining moment of fame... Not at all. I received 25 stitches in the front and five stitches in the back. That was my highlight in Grade 9.

Thankfully, for Grade 10, it was pretty uneventful. I started high school, and this meant a whole new school and teachers. I was able to meet friends who accepted me as I was. I still had many episodes in class where I stuttered, but I was able to get through it somehow, some way. I struggled still with my weight, but I had gotten used to how I looked and felt I couldn't do anything about it anyway. My best friend was a high achiever in school, never missing a class at all. She had high marks, which came easy for her. I, on the other hand, had to work hard for what I received and still couldn't beat her marks. This feeling of inadequacy grew in me to the point that I felt why bother. I was never going to get smarter, be more popular, and feel accepted. I stuttered. I was clumsy, and I definitely wasn't smart.

So...I jumped at the chance to get away from home to attend a private school in Saskatchewan. I wanted to have a fresh start with everything. The town where I lived had a Bible School as well as a high school, and the town was centered around these two schools, and it attracted people from all over the world. We all lived in dorms with "Leaders" that were in charge of us. Most of my roommates were great, but when you live with a bunch of other girls, there can be a lot of drama and a lot of law-breaking going on.

As much as this new experience was exciting, there were so many things that captured my attention, but I still felt insecure. I didn't feel I could ever measure up to the many others that came with money, popularity, looks, and smarts.

It's interesting...I went to a high school that taught about God and His goodness and how we are made in His likeness and image. Yet, I was ignoring all of that, and I chose not to make this a priority in my life. I just wanted to fit in, maybe be a bit popular, and yes, boys were always in the equation. I never felt connected with the weekly Bible studies that we did in our dorms or the discussions we had in class. Oh, how I wish I had a different focus! I possibly could have saved myself from future drama, pain, and heartache.

When I returned that next fall, I met a Bible School student shortly after starting. I thought he was so nice and caring, and we cliqued so quickly. We started dating, which, by the way, was kind of off bounds between a high school student and a Bible school student. But I didn't care. I felt wanted, loved, and I wasn't concerned about what rule I was breaking. I'm not sure how I got permission to go off campus and take a trip to his parents' place, about 3 hours away from where I was living. I was going to meet his parents and sister and spend some time alone together. After arriving at his parents' house, he drove me around the town, and I saw where he grew up. His parents had left the house with his sister, so we headed back to the house. We finally had some alone time. We talked for a bit, looked at old pictures, and held each other.

However, this intimacy developed into more touching and intimacy. I thought I had found love and acceptance, but the more he persisted in his passion towards me, I was really feeling uncomfortable and uneasy. What if his parents or sister walked in? What would they think of me? How could I face myself? I asked him to stop, and he wouldn't. I kept asking him, and he still wouldn't stop.

He forced me to do things I am not proud of, but he threatened he would tell everyone what we did if I didn't do what he asked. As I write this, and this was over 37 years ago, I still feel a bit of that pain and disgust still over what happened. It took me a long time before I was able to look in the mirror at myself. That beautiful piece of a child had been destroyed. I felt disgusting, worthless, and like a used piece of trash.

Life at school was very awkward. I avoided the cafeteria line when I knew the Bible school students were there. I tried to hide when we had to go to the chapel in the morning. I couldn't believe it. This was just the beginning of the year! The pain was hard to bear or even talk about it. It wasn't until I had finished high school, graduated, and was back at home that one evening while at the dinner table with my parents, and talking about school, this turned into a conversation of boyfriends. I am not sure of the words that were spoken, but when I felt confident enough that I could share what had happened, my father said to me, "Well, you should have picked better boyfriends." At the time, I was so angry that he blamed me for what had happened, that I had brought this up myself. Wow...that hurt. I thought I was not expecting that. Now, as I think back, I just feel that my dad just couldn't find the right words to say and said what he thought was the best.

I went to live with my sister only because I wanted a change from being at home. This was pretty cool. I lived in the basement and she was upstairs. We got along quite well, but she had her life and I had mine. I tried to hide my pain through drinking, drugs, and sex. Nothing seemed to work to make me feel loved and accepted except at the bar, or so I thought. Here is where I was popular when I was there. It was the bad-ass attitude I started developing, thinking I was unstoppable and no one could tell me what to do. That was a cover-up to the emptiness I felt. I felt trapped. I was spiraling further and further down this deep dark hole and there didn't seem to be a way out of it at all.

One night in the winter, I had come home from the bar. My sister wasn't home. I made sure of that. I wanted to end it all. I wanted to leave this cruel, hurtful world that had given me so much pain. I felt worthless, a nobody...So I sat on her front steps, hoping that I would freeze to death. It was quite cold outside, and I guess I was a chicken and copped out of this plan about an hour into it. I just couldn't do it. Something made me stop and go inside. Looking back now, I believe it was my fighting spirit within telling me to keep going, keep picking up your feet and moving forward.

Life kind of went on this way for a while of drinking, partying and not really caring about anything.... However, I still had the voice of my dad in my head, but this time, it was repeating the phrase that I have heard so many times over and over again; 'You better make something of yourself, get a certificate, get your schooling. `

SO I enrolled in nursing school and got accepted to Medicine Hat College. Here I could possibly escape rules and I was excited about another adventure. Oh yeah...I was going to school. Let's not forget that.

I did well in my studies but as nursing students are known for, drinking and partying are also in that mix. Ironically, the bar that we frequented was also kitty-corner to the church that I attended. How Ironic. I could drink on the weekend and go to Church on Sunday...What a great combination. Oh, I drank, smoked, did a bit of the nasty stuff...and partied hard. I didn't care about what I looked like or who I was with. I needed to let loose, and that is what I did. I didn't complete my studies here as I had a teacher say to me I wasn't cut out. Wow...what another blow to the ego.

Well, fast forward with my story. It wasn't until I finally met my husband of now 23 years that I finally felt loved, accepted and wanted. He didn't care that I struggled with stuttering and low self-esteem. He didn't care that I was raped. He didn't care about any of that. I'm not saying that he was insensitive because that is the farthest from the truth. He just chose not to let that be my focus or his. He was there to pick me up, encourage me and give me tips and pointers to get better. He was exactly what I needed to continue improving my overall health.

I did achieve my Nursing Degree in 2006 while working pretty well full time, studying online, moving to another province, living in a hotel, and raising two little kids.

But you know what… beyond all of this...My worth is not in the things that I have accomplished or attained. It is not in the titles that I have or the education that I have taken. My worth is in Jesus Christ, who has created us in God's Image. He loved me before I was created, thought of, and beyond measure. He was there at the beginning when I was really little, and stuttered at home. He was there when I was in school, getting teased by the kids. He was there during High School when I went 13 hours away from home to attend a private school. He was there when I was raped by my boyfriend at college, and at Bible school. He has been there through everything I have gone through. I just didn't realize it. I didn't allow him to give me the strength and courage to keep going. I was so wrapped up in my "life" that I didn't see that God was there. If I only called out to Him, He would've helped me. You know what? I am glad that I went through all of that. It has made me into who I am today. I have been able to help others who are going through similar things. My stuttering is way better today and I hardly notice it anymore. God has brought me through many storms and trials and is always there to pick me up.

He is gracious and merciful.

Here is where my life really started taking off. I became interested in knowing more about brain health, and how I could improve my own. Since having two head injuries, I wanted to learn all I could learn about how to make better decisions, live longer, be happier, and so much more. This knowledge would prove to be helpful when I became a mom. My third child was born with a cleft palate and lip and would then develop dilated cardiomyopathy. He suffered a head injury as well, as a toddler when he fell down the stairs when our stair gates were not fastened. I really didn't start putting things together until just recently. He struggled with fitting in, understanding simple and easy concepts, and needed one-on-one help. When I finished my brain health training, I assessed him and realized that because of the fall, he had suffered prefrontal cortex damage, which had contributed to his learning difficulties and behavioral outbursts. It made so much sense. I was able to identify the issue and also learn how to help him. I started him on "Attention Support" from www.brainmd.com, and it helped him decrease his attitude outbursts, focus more at school and be more attentive both in class and at home.

It was about five years after my third son was born that my aunt was diagnosed with Alzheimer's disease. She was a very bright woman, a teacher for many years, and a gifted individual, a mother, and a wife. It seemed like in a blink of an eye, her memory was gone, and she required more and more care until, eventually, her husband placed her into extended care for Alzheimer's clients. It's so sad to see how the mind can be greatly impacted when the connections are not working properly.

This sparked more of my passion to keep learning, teaching others how our brain works, why it is important to take care of it, and what we can do to protect it, change it, and keep it optimized.

I wanted to be a change maker.

I wanted to see people before they got to this space. I wanted to help others be all that they can be, live the life they want to, and consider alternate options for natural health. I started talking to others about other options, and I was encouraged to consider being a health coach.

My health education journey started first through my nursing education. I worked in various areas and took care of many different types of patients and clients with a wide spectrum of health issues and concerns. However, I wasn't given the opportunity to really spend the needed time to get to know them due to the craziness of the ward or clinical area.

I enrolled through the Institute of Integrative Nutrition (online program in NEW YORK, NY). This was a great program, I learned a lot and was refreshed on information I learned in nursing, but I still wanted more. I wanted to learn all that I could learn to help others in their lives, health and empower them to help others do the same.

I enrolled through Amen University for the Brain Certification Course, Brain Warriors Way, and Brain Thrive by 25 courses. I wanted to be so self-absorbed in all that I could learn about the brain, and I could change not only my own health and life but also those whom I love and care for.

I obtained a certificate as a Brain Health Coach and Trainer. It made me realize I can change my brain, I can make it better, and I can help others do the same. I can move forward and make my brain better despite the injuries I sustained through proper nutrition, exercise/movement, daily renewal of my mind and self-care techniques, and so much more.

It wasn't until I took part in the Daniel Plan at church that this passion for learning more about the brain really took off. If I could take my knowledge as a nurse, a holistic health coach, and combine it with brain health, I could really help others live the lives they have only dreamed of. I wanted to empower others to change their lives, change their brains and teach others to do the same.

I graduated in June of 2019 and started Radically Transformed Coaching.

We can truly move forward from whatever we have experienced, thought, dealt with, changed our brain, changed our health, and, of course, changed our life. We are not stuck with the brain that we have. We can make it better, and I can teach you how. We can move forward to protect our minds and prevent the 11 risk factors that steal our memory and mind.

Radically Transformed Coaching is a unique name. It is powerful in one way and transformational in another. Radically Transformed is how your brain can be radically transformed when you become a Warrior for the health of your brain, know your why to get healthy and do all that you can do to protect it. This is powerful. However, Radically Transformed is also how you can be radically transformed through the love and grace Jesus Christ has given us when we take up our crosses and follow Him when we acknowledge all that, He has done for us and all that He will do for us. He brings us through any trial, any heartache, and gives us all that we need in His time. Now, that is Transformational.

So, through much counseling and support, I have overcome these feelings and thoughts. I was able to work through my pain. I have been able to lose weight and still continue on that journey. I have to renew my mind daily to the reason why I am here on this earth, my purpose, why I am a mother, a wife, a friend, a sister, and a daughter. The imagery of a broken mirror is still here, but it is a reminder that I am loved, cherished, and valuable, and I am being transformed out of that brokenness.

As Joyce Meyer states, I am not where I want to be, but I definitely am not where I used to be. God has restored me and continually keeps molding and shaping me from a cracked pot to a beautiful gem.

My goal, as I mentioned at the beginning, is to be on 100 stages, to teach women who have gone through struggles how to get to the root of the pain and how to start taking one step forward. I was afraid to take that first step, but I did it. I was terrified I would get laughed at, but I did it. I am not where I want to be, but I am definitely not where I used to be. I want to show others that I have overcome and still continue to overcome stuttering. The first step was really hard, but it got easier and easier the more times I took the first step forward. You can do it too. I want women to feel empowered, loved, accepted, and valuable no matter what has happened in their lives. I want women to feel the beauty within themselves.

Krista McLellan

Inspiration – Becoming a single mom of two active daughters, I learned valuable lessons on how to be financially independent and run a business, all while being able to be involved with and available to my girls. Those lessons were hard-won, and my passion is to share them with other women so they can run their businesses with confidence. Money Making Mammas was created so we can connect with other women who want the same and have a place where we can find inspiration, support, resources for learning, and so much more! We are stronger together!

Connect with Krista:

https://www.instagram.com/moneymakingmammas/

https://www.facebook.com/moneymakingmammas/

https://www.linkedin.com/in/krista-mclellan-064a7013

Chapter 9

Money Making Mammas

By Krista McLellan

Looking down at my newborn baby girl, I knew I couldn't leave her. I had a hard time leaving my puppy to go to work; how would I ever be able to leave my baby? The journey to find a career that allowed me to have it all began then and there.

Let me introduce myself

I was raised by a single mom. My parents have been divorced for as long as I can remember. My mom worked full time and did my grandfather's books on the weekends. One of my earliest memories is being a little girl in my grandfather's trucking company office, sorting and counting change. This was where I learned how to track money like a boss and curse like a truck driver. Two skills that still serve me today.

Both of my parents remarried (a few times for my dad) and seemed to be in a competition over having more children, giving me a large family of about a dozen siblings collectively with the blended families. I was "blessed" with having several stepmothers throughout my life. Each of these very interesting women had an impact on me. One of the best lessons I learned from this part of my journey in life was how to not just "deal" with diverse personalities and situations but how to adapt and thrive in chaos. The downside of such a large family was that I sometimes felt invisible or forgotten. Ballet became my refuge. Something that was just mine and a place I could shine.

From Ballet to BoardRoom

The studio was my favorite place. When I needed to shut out the world, I practiced. I loved the disciplined repetition of barre work and the competition of being better than I was yesterday. Those lessons have been both a saving grace and a liability for me as an adult. When I'm under pressure, I work harder. I find the repetition and discipline of my work meditative.

Despite this ability to focus on something that makes me feel good, I struggle with never feeling good enough. When I was younger, I even broke up with my first boyfriend because I didn't feel I was good enough for him. I know I'm not alone in this because I've heard from so many women that can relate and have similar insecurities.

The ballet world can be cruel and had me at war with my body as I was naturally a little curvy. Yup, I got junk in the trunk. Enough to make it so my tutu didn't sit "nice and flat" like they thought it should. That was not desirable for ballet dancers at the time; not sure much has changed even today despite some of the positive changes.

Later, I was injured and had to put a hold on dancing which inadvertently caused weight gain, dimming my already poor self-confidence. This followed me into adulthood and hovers near on the daily. Imagine trying to run a business and not having the confidence to ask to get paid or set boundaries, so you don't get taken advantage of. I can tell you it's not a good mix, as any business consultant will tell you. After trying to hide my body, to try and blend into the background for most of my life, learning that it's ok to take up space, have a voice, ask for what you want, and even not be ashamed of my curves has been a long road that I still travel-every day.

Oh Mamma!

My first business started by watching other people's kids so I could get paid for staying home with my own babies. I dropped out of college after my freshman year and got married, thinking that was how to become an independent adult. My husband had a job with Raytheon he was laid off from but had the opportunity to realize his childhood dream of being a firefighter. Unfortunately, being a firefighter in our tiny town did not pay well. Here I was, a new mom with no degree or skill set, knowing daycare would cost more than I would earn at a regular job. This quandary of figuring out how to be home with my daughter yet still contribute financially was the motivation behind my entrepreneurial journey. This struggle took me into a world of business ownership when being a female business owner wasn't the thing to do.

Daycare Daze

My friends and family often joked that I ran a home daycare. I was not known for enjoying small children that weren't my own. My determination won out, and I made this "my business," so ultimately, the drive to succeed prevailed. As it turned out, I not only liked keeping the daycare's books, but I was really good at it and preferred it over the day-to-day running of the daycare.

My tax preparer counseled me that I surely missed my calling and asked If I wanted to earn extra money helping others with their books. Making money doing something I love? YES, please! I dipped my toe in the waters of bookkeeping and took on one of his clients. He paired me with another daycare owner who needed training and mentorship in learning how to do her books. This new path was intimidating, to say the least, but this mom is no quitter, and I put my all into everything I do. Almost instantly, it hit me; this was what I was meant to do.

Have you ever heard someone say bookkeeping is fun? I found bookkeeping and helping others succeed just that! The connection with other women running their own businesses not only sparked a light in me, but it was also the gasoline for the flame! Onward to the journey into entrepreneurship.

Next Came the Naysayers

I was told I couldn't, that I wasn't an accountant, that no one would take me seriously. In fact, my sanity was questioned because I failed math not once but twice before I dropped out of college. Who did I think I was starting a bookkeeping business? I am grateful my dad taught me from a young age that I could do anything I set my mind to. He would jokingly tease me and say, "Don't you know you can't do that -you're a girl?" My dad loved getting me used to fighting back. Overcoming the influence of other people who didn't support my vision or believe in me wasn't easy. It was a huge responsibility to have someone rely on me, to learn to use a computer and software, never mind how to give the CPA the information he wanted, and to figure out how to charge for my time. But who doesn't love and actually NEED a good challenge sometimes?

The issue of not being taken seriously was a major obstacle in the beginning. Firstly, I knew I had to start off undercharging until I gained experience and proved myself. In one of my first board meetings, I was the only female and was asked to "fetch coffee and take notes," even though I was there to present the financials.

I have learned how to deal with the occasional Neanderthal thinking. In fact, I have become a pro at educating those mindsets on modern thinking and the role of today's women. Presenting myself in a way that I am seen as an advisor and proving my value in that capacity typically speaks for itself.

Working with business owners is surprisingly intimate. I have found that the skills I used in previous roles have come into play as a mentor. I nurture my clients, listen to and encourage them through tough times to help them believe in themselves. I help them to set goals for their business that will benefit their family and maintain focus when they get off course. My holistic approach to business brings peace to their business which equates to more harmonious family life.

For five years, I ran my daycare while building a clientele. The time came when I knew it was time to shut down the daycare and focus on the business. At this time, my then-husband preferred me to be home and wasn't enthusiastic (or overly supportive) about me going to clients' offices. You can imagine this overwhelming skepticism and what a challenge in itself it was. I had to prove not only to others but to myself that I could do it.

The limiting belief of not being good enough or smart enough is something so many of us struggle with. Because of this, I am a strong advocate for professional enrichment to improve abilities, evolve, and do what might be uncomfortable for you. I have been blessed to be aligned with amazing mentors who have helped me and strive to give back to others the support I had.

Have Laptop, Will Travel

I am grateful that I was able to learn how to be self-reliant. Creating E&M Bookkeeping would be what saved our little family. Shortly after my husband and I separated, he was diagnosed with cancer. I jumped in and referred to it as water under the bridge. He was my daughter's dad and my friend, so I knew what I had to do.

Not long after Scott got sick, we found out there was no disability or social security insurance to support him or us. If I hadn't started my business, we would have been destitute. My little bookkeeping business gave me the flexibility to take care of him as well as my children.

I had created the work-life balance I so desperately craved when my girls were little. This arrangement assured me I could take Scott to Boston every week for his treatments and work remotely onsite. I brought my computer with me, worked on files, and answered emails and phone calls from the waiting rooms. I have been able to work and bill for my time in the dance studio, waiting rooms, at soccer tournaments between games, and anywhere else I found myself with downtime. I took that downtime and turned it into billable hours. Taking advantage of these pockets of time made it so that when I was home, I could actually be home and present to help with homework or hear about their day.

Independence Day

Learning to live on my own meant teaching my children about money and budgeting. They needed to know where our money came from and where it needed to go. My girls were 8 and 11 when their dad got sick, and our life dramatically changed. The three of us decided together what was a need versus a want.

They chose to give up things like cable and Christmas presents so we could keep our home.

Money management and cash flow were not only my business but a critical tool for survival. We all made do with hand-me-downs instead of new clothes, and the cold New England winters meant putting on extra layers because we needed to keep the thermostat low to conserve heating oil.

The girls learned at an early age to earn their own spending money as I provided the necessities, but they had to pay for their extras. The first year was the hardest. I remember not having enough money for new tires. One of the hardest but best memories was of the gift cards the girls had been given for Christmas from members of their dad's fire department. They gave me their Christmas gift cards to buy tires. Such a bittersweet moment. It was so hard to take their money but seeing them proudly offering to be part of the solution filled me with incredible pride. It was the three of us against the world, and we were determined to win together.

I was a single mom of two very active girls, and my dream of being able to get my kids to and from school, be a hands-on, full-time mom, AND earn enough money to support us had come true. Money was tight, but the three of us decided that time with them, being able to go to soccer games and dance rehearsals, track meets, field hockey games, and being involved was more important than material things.

Once they were old enough to drive and didn't need me to be their chauffeur, I was finally free to grow my business. I had intentionally kept it small enough to handle mom hours, but now that they were more independent, there was nothing holding me back. I had made a name for myself and had a waitlist of referrals but not enough time in the day.

Up Up and Away!

It was time to learn a new technology – cloud-based accounting. My eldest daughter Elizabeth dragged me into it, kicking and screaming because I don't love change and, at the time, lacked the confidence to migrate to this new platform. She was going to school to be an accountant and had grown up working in the business with me. She knew how my brain worked and knew that I needed to evolve to continue to grow. Previously, I tried implementing technology unsuccessfully, so she had to convince me to try again, and it became one of the best decisions I ever made.

I was able to take on more work right from home, saving on gas and wardrobe money, as well as being more efficient overall. This has created a domino effect of growth with the need to hire and train help. I've even had to offload some of the clients that weren't a good fit for me as I grew. Thankfully, training other women have given me plenty of referral options.

My youngest daughter Emily helped me create my first website. She also challenged me and then taught me how to go as paperless as possible, showing me ways of safely sharing information. She mentored me with what she had learned in school.

Mamma Said There'd Be Days Like This

Life has definitely presented sometimes painful learning opportunities. I learned the value of having a non-compete contract when someone I trained went after my clients. There was also a client that I thought was a friend. He knew I had just lost the girls' dad and wasn't in the best financial position. He not only used my time but intruded on other clients' time, causing a negative impact on my business and an even worse impact on my cash flow when he refused to pay me for my invested time.

Not budging and taking him to court taught me the value of a good contract and even better record keeping. Did I win the case? You're damn straight I did. The judge was impressed that I had such excellent supporting documentation of our emails, texts, and phone calls proving my work. Teaching those I mentor how to protect themselves is a huge priority as there are always those unkind and selfish people who will try to take advantage of others. Sadly, it is part of the world we live in.

The She Shed

By 2019, I had a national clientele with support staff. However, I was running it from my kitchen table and the extra office of one of my primary clients. It was awkward to meet other clients there or in my kitchen, to say the least. I looked into renting an office or repurposing my garage into an office, but neither seemed like the best use of funds.

Along came "The She Shed." I bought a prefab shed, electrified it, insulated it, and put in a split HVAC unit to create an office at my house but yet away from my house. It enabled me to have a quiet place to work, a place clients can come and feel comfortable discussing business.

Support staff and interns (yup, I even have the occasional accounting student as an intern) have a great place to come when they want to meet in person. I have enough space to be organized and a big enough desk for two monitors to reduce the need for printing anything out.

When the pandemic hit and my kids were both going to school remotely, I was even more appreciative that I had a place where

I could work without the background noise of kids, a dog, and real life.

Dream Big! Shine That Light!

So many of us live in fear and don't move forward, letting our trepidation of the unknown hold us back. We crack open the door to an opportunity and then take a step back because of our anxiety about what's going to come flying out. Taking that next step and shining a light helps us to see that scary thing was way bigger in our imagination than it ever was in reality. Ignorance is not bliss. It is so much harder to stumble around with a blindfold on, trying not to trip over what we can't see.

I want to help people stand in their power. Having to face this world with my children alone forced me to do the things that I thought were too hard or that I couldn't do. With the help of friends, mentors, and advisors, I conquered obstacles that seemed impossible, and guess what? They ended up not being as hard as I thought. I learned I could do way more than I thought I was capable of, and this helped me have the confidence to accomplish even more.

There's nothing so big that we can't do it **one step at a time**. We just need somebody to either show us how, stand beside us, or back us up. By taking baby steps, we accomplish smaller goals which make the next step easier because we gain more confidence not only in the process but in ourselves. Helping people change their negative self-talk that perpetuates failure into confidence that builds success is transforming.

Just because something is uncomfortable or unknown doesn't mean we can't do it. I truly believe we aren't given more than we can handle. It's ok to fall down and get back up because that's how we get stronger and learn you don't have to do it alone.

There are people who will help you, that have done it, that will show you how they did it, and will give you tips and tricks.

Find your mentor. It's well worth it!

Money Making Mammas

If I knew then what I know now – I wouldn't change a thing.

Becoming a mom changed my life. In 2000 being an entrepreneur and a mom wasn't really heard of, but now it even has a name-momtrepreneur. I decided to plan my life around my kids, and it was the best decision I ever made. I have been truly blessed with clients that have become friends, and the women I have trained have become like family. Helping others succeed has become my favorite part of the business.

I don't believe in being a victim or living in fear. Your obstacles don't need to hold you back or own you but can propel you forward instead. By changing my perspective from focusing on what I **don't** like in my life to focus on what I **want**, then creating a plan to get it, I have been able to manifest my dreams into reality. If I can do it, so can you!

Paying forward the mentorship I was blessed with has become a passion of mine. Working with other women to help them start their businesses, take control of their finances, and write their next chapter sparks that fire in me. Encouraging other women to let their light shine and providing them the benefit of the lessons I learned (the hard way) has turned into a community of Money Making Mammas.

The privilege of watching women learn to stand in their power is both exhilarating and humbling. Wanting to be moms and to still be financially independent IS possible. One of the many things I challenge the women I have trained is to ask themselves,

"How do we stand in our power financially if we give that up to our partners and rely on them to support us?"

I learned the hard way how much power and independence I had given up when my girls' dad passed away. He paid the bills from his bank account with his email and passwords that I had no access to. I had to let my electricity get shut off in order to start a new account in my name. My mortgage went into foreclosure, so I could get it moved into my contact details to pay it. Learning how to mow my lawn, fix blown fuses, and run my snowblower wasn't my idea of fun. I cried and resented having to do it, but I did it, and I learned.

The light dawned when a dear friend of mine helped me get my head on straight and said to stop seeing these things as problems and start seeing them as blessings. That was an epiphany. I went from seeing myself as a victim to realizing I was writing my next chapter and that I could be the heroine instead. From that day forward, every obstacle has indeed turned into an opportunity to grow, achieve, and, most importantly, to teach my daughters that we are ok on our own.

Today, I am more in love with my business than ever. Helping others live their dream fans that flame I so often talk about. Here I am, a college dropout who failed math, fought (still does) social anxiety, and I'm running a successful business working with other Money Making Mammas. Aspiring them to connect with more champions, find supportive and loving partners as I have, surround themselves with like-minded women, and live in a community of support.

My community of Money Making Mammas (moneymakingmammas.com) can help you believe in yourself and make those dreams a reality. We have a great support group on Facebook and collaborate with some boundless online resources. Connect with us, share your story, and become part of something that is bigger than the power of one.

Nick Gemmell

After 23 years in the welding trade and 18 years in the Pipeline Industry, Nick knew there was a better way to live and, through his own Personal Development Journey, is more committed than ever to helping families make their dreams a reality. From welder to rig welder, to inspector, to Construction Manager for a major Pipeline Distributor in North America has given me a unique set of talents and the resilience to overcome anything.

Connect with Nick:

https://www.pipedreamcapital.com/

https://www.linkedin.com/in/nickgemmell/

https://www.instagram.com/nick.gemmell79/

Chapter 10

Making Your Pipe Dreams a Reality

By Nick Gemmell

My business:

Pipe Dream Solution

Who Am I?

I am Nick Gemmell.

Born and raised in Lethbridge, AB, the windy city!!

I started in the welding trade back in 1998, where I aspired to be a rig welder.

For those that do not know that world, a rig welder is a welder with his own welding truck. I started that business in 2004.

I was a one-man show now responsible for finding contracts, having my own insurance, and carrying my own overhead.

This was extremely difficult and stressful when you have never had to take on any of the headaches. All I knew was how to push through adversities, and I believe I did very well.

The problem with that, and I will get to that a little later, is that it wears on you when that is your world, day in and day out.

I was married in 2003 to a beautiful and talented woman whom I had two kids with.

When we found out about the first pregnancy was when I had the bright idea to start my company. I freaked out knowing what I made as a shop welder in Southern Alberta, and I heard of all these opportunities out in the oil patch, so it was then I made the leap into starting this new venture of being a rig welder.

Once I made the leap from commercial to the oilfield, you could imagine that now I am working further and further away from home and for longer and longer durations.

There were times when I remember my first long stint up north, in 2009, where I worked away for 56 days, which up until that point, was the longest I had ever worked away from home. During that job, I went from not drinking at all to drinking more and more as time went on.

Now just think about that for a moment….

You are married, have loved ones…now close your eyes and put yourself in a state where you do not physically see them for a week….

Let alone for 56 days.

Like, are you fucking kidding me!?!?

Without even taking a second look at what was going on around me, I was stuck.

I was stuck in this Oilfield Lifestyle and just going with the flow, whatever that looked like.

I knew I needed a change, and in 2012, I decided that I wanted to be a pipeline inspector.

With a back that had been injured in a curling incident (yes, I could hear you snicker from here as you read that), a curling incident, a pipeline inspector seemed like a logical next step.

I was then thrown into a world that I knew, but there was so much to learn, and the only way to learn was by being thrown into the fire.

Excelling at dealing with CHAOS was my MO.

This served me well, and I was asked to be a Construction Manager at a major Oil and Gas distributor in 2014.

At the time, I was the youngest CM at the company and felt a ton of pressure to perform.

This was where I believe I started to disconnect from my wife as a way to protect myself from the pressures that I was allowed to consume me in order to keep operating at that high level of expectations.

Due to the downturn in 2016, I was asked to go back to welding inspecting, and this was where my ego took a hit. A depression set in that helped fuel a fire in me to push harder than I ever had in a body transformation that ended up consuming me.

With less projects to go to and more stress of not having the money we used to while transitioning into a lifestyle of taking over the in-law's golf course, I 100% disconnected fully from my relationship with my wife and hid in Lethbridge while making excuses to not come home to our new house in British Columbia when she needed me the most.

See, what I have found is the brain is an amazing thing; it can either work for you or against you.

While all I wanted to do was provide an amazing life for my wife and kids, I allowed this lifestyle to turn me into a disconnected asshole that was only worried about a paycheck and not enjoying life at all.

While on the outside, I was the life of the party.

Always the one who everyone wanted to go on golf trips with because of the FUCKS NO GIVEN attitude that I brought to the table, and all at the same time, I was dying inside.

All of the birthdays, anniversaries, special moments of the kids that I never saw and will never get back, the friends left behind, and all the inside jokes that I fly straight over my head finally caught up to me.

I have been addicted to so many things in my life to sedate: Booze, gambling, weight training, dieting, and who can't forget golf.

Now some may say: How can you be addicted to weight training and golf!?!?

Well, what I have found is anything that takes me away from the present moment, I will use to sedate myself.

In seeking sedation and instant gratification, I do not need to deal with anything that is going on around me.

An hour and a half at the gym…

5hrs at the golf course….

Eating every 2hrs to keep me distracted….

Now, in the right frame of mind, these things can be a release, a good thing, but when your headspace is where all you know is how to be away at work…

Eat….

Sleep…

Do it again…

What the FUCK do you think is going to happen???

Between so many years of life on the road and away from my loved ones, I forgot who I was; I forgot what made me attractive to my spouse in the first place, and, worst of all, I forgot how to have fun.

This is a recipe for disaster that so many in the oil and gas industry have to either choose to navigate or many don't, and their families suffer the same fate.

This leads me to my next chapter in life, where my wife served me with divorce papers in 2018. Months after our separation when I was in on a pipeline project in Northern BC.

Even though I was seeing someone else whom she did not know about, I was served these papers seemingly out of nowhere even though we were separated.

This was how disconnected from reality I was, and I fucking lost it.

I lost my mind, and I was eventually moved from a project I was working on. On to another one where I later found out it was due to my negativity.

MY NEGATIVITY!?!?

I was always the person who held his shit together no matter what was going on.....I thought.

For the next project I got sent to, I ended up being the first person let go when layoffs started, whereas the previous winter with this same spread, I was one of the last inspectors on the project.

This just showcases how you are only as good as your last project, and we in the industry are disposable, so you better be on your best at all times.

For years I suppressed everything into my big toe, and this was the result.

Even then, I didn't decide to start to make a change after a counseling session where I tried to get my ex to join in a couples counseling session, and when she didn't show, the counselor and I started to talk about me.

What I neglected to tell you before is that I had a rough couple of months sitting in the PIT of suicidal thoughts and even a few calls for help where I threatened to actually follow through with these thoughts to my ex. To this day, I do not think I would have ever followed through with these, but it scared the SHIT out of me enough that I thought I should ask for help.

It was during these few counseling sessions where my ex did not show up that I started to deal with the pain of all that had transpired over the past nine months since she left me and wanted a divorce; where it started to come to light in discussions with the therapist where a light bulb came on and I realized I was an addict. Even though my behavior was pretty low-key in terms of actions, the motives behind most of the things that I have done have come down to wanting and feeling the need to sedate and remove myself from the situation.

I started to recall family dinners where I would throw a fit because friends would call and ask me to go golfing, and I would rather leave a nice family dinner, and, when I didn't get my own way, I would make it known that I was not happy.

All the embarrassment, guilt, and shame all started to flow through me all at once because I was allowing it. I had no idea how to deal with these thoughts and emotions. My head absolutely wanted to explode, and I finally made the decision to do something about it and not sit in this PIT any longer.

That was when I decided to go to rehab. In my mind, it was not for drugs or alcohol, but I just did not FEEL ANYTHING anymore. It was the weirdest realization of my life, and I just ran with it.

My mental health was declining by the day, and I realized no one was coming to save me, so I hopped on a plane to Thailand and went to HOPE Rehab Facility; and this was the single best idea of my life.

I decided to go to this particular facility because it was not clinical but spiritual.

No, not religious but SPIRITUAL.

I learned mindfulness, I learned meditation, I learned the power of writing and journaling, but most of all, I learned to love myself again and figure out why I was so ALL or NOTHING.

These were the absolute best two months of my life, and I was spending them with alcoholics and drug addicts from all over the world from different backgrounds and vocations. It was here I realized that I was NOT better than anyone and started to see the world again from a different lens; A lens of love and compassion again. My kids did not deserve their parents to divorce and a father to be disconnected. This experience started to fuel a fire inside me to want to start helping others that may be going through this same experience, even though I had just started this journey of healing myself.

It was then I was reintroduced to my friend Dr. Ryan P. Doyle of Victoria, BC, after living together nearly 20 years prior. I was always following him on Facebook and kind of would skip over him instead of listening to his videos.

You know...one of those guys who I was jealous of. On the outside, he seemed very successful and had his shit together with the good-looking family. One day about 50 days after my 60 at the rehab facility, I stopped and listened to what he had to say, and I literally said, "What the FUCK??? He is describing me!"

What he was actually describing, though, was his life and his experiences of nearly burning his life down by the use of drinking, triathlons, and using business as a reason to hide from his wife and kids.

So, an entirely different field. The man was in Chiropractic. How the FUCK could his life be similar to mine?!?!

Well, I decided to reach out to him to ask him what he was doing. What he told me was a system he was head coach of in the Men of Iron and their philosophies, and I was immediately drawn to it. What had me intrigued was the aspect of this program of the ability of MEN HELPING MEN.

So a lot of the tools that I learned in rehab were what the basis of the program was on, and I absolutely fell in love with the model and dove right in.

This would have been approximately one year from when COVID would start reaping havoc over the world, and I am so grateful to have already started down my coaching journey with this.

You see, I was already used to isolation, so when projects were getting canceled, and I was now forced to be home because of this global pandemic, I dove right into starting to refine my message and hammering social media with my REAL and RAW voice that I was starting to find.

The scary part of putting my message of standing up for yourself as a man and taking your life into your own hands in the oilfield was the people I was trying to reach. They are very vocal people; if they like something, they like it, and when they don't, they will murder you with words and negativity. The problem I was facing, though, was that there was nothing....crickets. No one was commenting or saying shit.

Ever since I realized that part of my people, I knew I was on to something. But as vulnerable as I was and had nothing coming back positive or negative, I just tweaked and tweaked my messaging, all while staying consistent and ruthless with the messaging and consistency of my posting.

As much as I wanted this to be my full-time business, I knew I had a long road ahead of me, and lucky for me, I have been able to get some work in the maintenance side of pipelines. What this also has given me is exposure and time.

Exposure to more people on their phones than usual.

Time, as I have not been as busy as usual with my REAL JOB in the pipeline.

What this TIME and EXPOSURE has allowed me to do was to tap into a market where NO ONE has ever dared to venture.

I am committed to helping men in the oilfield and the trades to give them the space and facilitate the change they say they want and really THRIVING at this oilfield lifestyle in all areas of their lives.

I pivoted my sole focus on the oilfield so these other men could choose to continue to live this lifestyle, like myself, for many different reasons but be able to:

-have a body that works

-a connection to themselves

-relationships that work,

-and a business and bank account they can be proud of.

In this business, so many of us seem to sit back and wait for the next OIL BOOM to come to save us.

The reality is NO ONE IS COMING TO SAVE US, and we are the master of our fate, and we are the captain of our soul.

So what COVID has been able to do for me is to be able to create the space I needed to be able to pivot and shove my message into the face of anyone who would listen.

I am not doing this for financial gain, even though, in full disclosure, I want this as my sole source of income in the very near future, and I do not want to work with just anyone.

I WANT TO WORK WITH PEOPLE WHO ACTUALLY WANT RESULTS AND NOT EXCUSES.

In today's society of inclusion and participation trophies, as a MAN, there is no second best for you to not play full out in this game of life, and without strong MEN, families, and our children do not stand a chance in this world.

So many people during COVID have realized what they were doing was not working but do not have the systems, tools, and network to be able to facilitate the change they are now wanting to work towards.

I help teach a system that facilitates the clients learning to HAVE IT ALL, and the testimonials speak for themselves.

Now as much as I do not want to go back to Oil and Gas at this time, I know this is a process, and I need to fund this new business off the PIPE DREAM SOLUTION somehow, and systems are getting implemented to be able to work and grow this new business full time.

I am also working on a Pipe Dream CORPORATE Solution that will allow employees at Oil and Gas Corporations the ability to live their best lives and deal with the shit in between their ears on a daily basis making these companies who use my system of uses actionable items, based on your values and life's mission to be able to push you forward helping make TEAMS MORE PRODUCTIVE AND SAFER.

What I have found is when people are attached to their WHY and their VALUES, they are more fulfilled and make better decisions.

This revelation could only have been found through my own BREAKDOWN to BUILD UP to BREAKTHROUGH.

I live this way of life-based on 90-day outcomes in my FITNESS, FULFILMENT, FAMILY, AND FINANCES, and being ruthlessly committed to teaching other men in the industry how to do the same is my mission.

Without my wife leaving and COVID, none of this would have been possible, and I would be waiting for the next OIL BOOM, like most of North America.

Even if that is your focus, you may want to consider this program so you can make the most of your time away.

My advice to other entrepreneurs in either the Oil/Gas space or in general is to set meaningful and specific targets in all areas of their lives every 90 days. Learn their values and develop a mission statement for themselves and their businesses, create daily habits based around those values and 90 days targets while returning and reporting on a weekly basis as to what is working and what they can leverage while pulling ONE URGENT item from their pending list.

Is sound impossible???

Enough with the SEDATION, and INSTEAD, it is time for you to make your PIPE DREAM A REALITY.

You can find me all over Social media to get your daily dose of motivation and give yourself a mental check of what you

#LEGACYDRIVEN #PIPEDREAMSOLUTION #PIPEDREAM #MENOFIRON

Nick Gemmell

Pipe Dream Solution

Wendie Holbrook

Wendie Holbrook is a solo mom to one amazing and beautiful daughter who has been her "why" for the past 13 years. Her daughter, Hannah, has been the most important reason for her fighting through some of the toughest times she has had to face, including domestic violence, to get into a position of owning her own business and moving toward the goal of owning a home in the middle of nowhere and having a small farm and doing life on her own terms.

Wendie hopes her daughter will be able to model what she has done and come out tough enough to take on the world and build her own dreams, no matter what they may be. If Wendie can encourage just one person with her story, it is all worth it! Go after your dreams, no matter what obstacles are in the way. Push through those obstacles and carry on until your dreams are fully realized! You only get one life; make it the best one ever!

Connect with Wendie:

https://virtually-yours.ca/

https://www.facebook.com/VirtuallyYoursAdmin

Chapter 11

Beyond the Brokenness

By Wendie Holbrook

There comes a time when you must draw a line in the sand and decide what is best for you and for those you love.

You see, I had just finally gotten out.

I had finally escaped from the man others termed "my husband," but whom I referred to as my abuser. I had been physically and emotionally abused, trapped, and controlled and was finally able to escape and return to Canada after spending the first year and a half in the United States with my daughter after she had been born.

My daughter and I then stayed with my brother and his wife for a month until I could come up with enough money to cover a security deposit and the first month's rent on an apartment. After I finally had enough money together, we moved into a one-bedroom apartment. My daughter slept with me as she was still little, and in time, when I could afford to, we would move to a bigger place so she could have her own room.

We had no furniture. No couch, no table, no chairs, no bed, no drawers, no pots and pans, and no dishes. We had nothing but the clothes we packed back to Canada and some borrowed sheets and blankets we used on the inflatable mattress we slept on for close to six months. It turns out I had been paying for a storage unit for 16 months while in the United States, assuming my furniture, including a brand-new mattress, amongst other belongings, were in there, and when I returned to Canada, I would be able to move those items back into my new apartment.

Not so.

It turns out my "husband" discarded all my belongings without my knowledge except for a fan, laundry basket, and a few boxes of books.

I had to start over, and I was so thankful for being given the opportunity to return to the administrative position I had held in the past so I could support my daughter and myself. I needed to be able to earn enough to pay my own rent, full-time daycare, groceries, and the other usual bills while receiving little to no additional support at that time.

My days began with me dropping my daughter off at daycare around 7:30 AM and then starting my one-and-a-half-hour commute to downtown Vancouver. I drove nearly three hours a day going to work and back and did this for nearly five years. I would see my daughter for an hour in the evening when I would bathe, feed, and tuck her into bed, only to collapse and do it all again the following day.

At one point, I decided during a Christmas break I had enough of the commuting and putting in requests to get time off for Christmas and a week during the summer when my daughter's daycare was closed.

I started to look through the classifieds for another opportunity. It was nice to just look and see what else was out there without having the pressure of having no work over my head. It was then I came across an ad for a virtual assistant.

I honestly had no idea what a virtual assistant was. It was clear from the ad this was a "work from home" opportunity, which did have me a little nervous as those types of jobs normally involved licking and stamping envelopes or something along those lines.

I read the details of the requirements for the position, and they were all skills I possessed from my previous positions as an Administrative Assistant and an Office Manager. I was excited about this job opportunity and decided I would revamp my resume and apply for the position.

Soon after applying, I heard back from the company that was headhunting for the position. The woman who called me did a short little interview over the phone and said I met all the criteria of what they were looking for and asked if I would like to come in for an interview.

It was tricky as I did not want to let my employer know I was looking elsewhere. I valued my position and had a great deal of respect for the woman with who I was working, so I managed to do the interview a time late in the day, so I would not miss work.

The lady informed me there were plenty of people applying for the position as it was offering a very good salary and benefits and, of course, was virtual. I tried not to get my hopes up too much as it really seemed like a once-in-a-lifetime type of opportunity. Still, I kept dreaming of what it would be like working from home and being able to spend more time with my daughter.

Then I got the second call from the head-hunting company asking if I would be able to come in for a second in-person interview.

Of course, I could! I decided I was going to land this position *no matter what.*

This time I would be meeting with the owner of the business hiring for the position and the head-hunting lady as well. I dressed my best. I showed up early, and when I was leaving the interview, the owner of the company hiring walked me to the elevator and asked if she could give me a hug. Somehow that left me feeling pretty good about how the interview went.

Then the call came. The job was mine!

I shopped for a desk and what I would need to work from home. I was ecstatic. The hard part was telling my current employer I would be leaving. She had helped me an enormous amount when I was just coming out of the worst situation of my entire life. She was there not only as my boss but as my friend through some dark times had shown my daughter and me a lot of concern and love.

My boss put together an amazing going-away lunch for me and gave me the most beautiful bouquet of flowers I have ever seen.

My heart was full.

It was so very bittersweet leaving, but it was another transition in life that would offer good things for my daughter and me, and that was what was most important.

It was incredible being able to work from home. I would take my daughter to school and return home for my day, and this new position enabled me to spend more time in the afternoon with my daughter going to the park and playing. Just that alone was amazing.

After nearly a year, my new employer advised me things were rather tight financially, and she was not sure she would be able to keep me on.

I was devastated and a little scared.

I came up with an offer for her to work as a contractor and let go of their benefits. This would save her the cost of the benefits and all the other costs that go with having an employee.

She agreed. What a relief.

A few months later, I was confronted with an opportunity to move about seven hours north of where we were. My brother and his wife were relocating, and I wanted to explore the possibility of relocating to where they were going. I started to look and see what there was in the way of housing where they were moving. Rent was not too expensive, and I found an opportunity where my daughter and I could rent a cute house on acreage.

Since I was working virtually, it really did not matter too much where we were located as long as there was access to the internet, and we could remain close to family, which was important for not only me as a single parent but my daughter as well so she could have her aunt, uncle and cousins close.

The one concern, however, was what would happen to us if something happened to this contract work. I decided I needed to have a serious discussion with my client as she was my only client and my only source of income at that time. I told her about where I would be moving, and the fact it was a small town with little in the way of options for work should something go sour with her business.

She assured me, "I was her girl," and I had work with her as long as I wanted.

With that settled, I started the process of paying a security deposit on the new place and renting a truck to move. I was so excited about this new place, so far away from all the busyness of where we were. It was a cute little home on acreage, which means we could have some of the things we had been dreaming about, like a small homestead.

With some of my personal issues settled with my daughter's father, a home secured for us, and my current income guaranteed, we loaded the moving truck and headed north.

It was like a breath of fresh air being in a new town. People were super friendly, and it was exciting to have new opportunities on the horizon.

As we settled into life in our new place, I continued to work with my sole client. It was summertime, so when my day was done at my desk, we could ease into the yard, and my daughter and I could play and work on some projects together. I built her a swing which she loved, and we took every opportunity we could to go on some walk or adventure with our dog.

As summer rolled into the fall, I continued to have full-time hours with my client and the routine of taking my daughter to school in the morning, about five minutes away from our home and returning to work, and then being able to pick her up at the end of her school day was great.

Then came October.

I received the call one morning three months after moving to our new home. It was about nine in the morning, and my client called to advise me that day would be my last day with her. I could hardly understand what she was saying to me as I sat there feeling like the floor was coming out from under me. There was no real reason, and she told me her daughter was finishing school and she would be working for her. She was prepared to pay an amount to cover the short notice she had given me as a type of severance, reminding me that she did not owe that to me.

I had no other clients and therefore no other income coming in, no child support yet, although I had a court order for it, and we had just moved to this small town with little to nothing in the way of work.

How would I pay the rent? The car payment, which was close to $800 a month? The utilities? The hydro alone was $600 a month. Groceries? My daughter's school?

I was sick to my stomach.

I have never been one for letting a tough situation get me down. I am strong. I had survived a dangerous domestic violence situation and brought my daughter and me this far. My former boss had told me she could not believe I had been through what I had been through, and she knew even after I had left my husband, there were still many days of hell to deal with because of him, and yet she said I was always smiling and positive. Even one day after my husband had been up to visit my daughter and he had once again attacked me, I still showed up to work. Still smiling, or at least doing my best to. She remarked it must be my faith that has carried me and said nothing else would get someone through what I had been through while still being optimistic, and she was right. I had just survived battle after battle in my home and in the Supreme Court and a trial successfully, and nearly all on my own.

This was just another battle I had to come out on top of, and I had to do it, not just for me but for my daughter as well.

What I did know for sure was I was not going to go back to a "9-5" job only to sit in some office making minimum wage while having no time with my daughter and barely making ends meet.

That was just not happening.

So, I allowed myself the rest of the day to grieve this loss because the next day was a new day.

I had come to realize working for myself and calling the shots on what days I would work, what type of work I enjoyed doing, what hours I would work, when I would take my vacation, and when I could just allow my daughter or me a "sick day," was important to me. I was not letting that go.

I was not going backward.

So, where to begin?

I decided to consider what it was I enjoyed most in terms of tasks and how I could market those services and tried to determine from there who my ideal client was. In my recent contract work, I was working with a lot of realtors, and having a virtual assistant makes a lot of sense in the real estate world. Realtors are on the go all the time. Many have an office, and some don't, but having an assistant who does not require an office to work out of, has their own computer and related equipment, and who is contracting their services makes a lot of sense to not just a realtor, for example, but really for anyone with a small business.

Just saving the cost of paying employee benefits and source deductions for tax purposes alone is reason enough to contract administrative services out, but add in the cost of not paying a bookkeeper to keep track of those costs, pay for an office, computer, and related equipment, sick days, vacation, and the list goes on.

This was my platform for marketing my services. How could I save "you" money?

In a very short order, I designed a website for myself and ordered business cards for express delivery. I set up an e-mail platform so I could market my services online by reaching out to the local realtors and small business owners with some e-mail marketing. I went to all the local real estate office websites and gathered e-mail addresses. I looked up small businesses and got their contact information, and when my business cards arrived, I went into town every single day and went from business to business, asking to meet the owner of the business or if I could meet with any realtors who happened to be in the office. I handed out business cards and explained my services.

What I did find is that most of the people I was meeting had the same look in their eyes. That deer in the headlight type of look when I used the words "virtual assistant." They could not understand having someone doing their work virtually. What you must also understand is that in this particular small town, most people still do not have any idea about how to do online banking. They were about two to five years behind the times.

In fact, it was because of this type of situation I applied and was chosen for a spot speaking at a TEDx event through the University of Northern British Columbia in 2018. The topic was about the future, and I wanted to speak about how the future looks in terms of work and how I thought most people would be working virtually in the years to come.

I was extremely fortunate and blessed during this time to have an amazing landlord who was extremely understanding of my situation. He also was an owner of a local business and was very gracious in extending me contract work during this time while I was building up my client base again. It meant having to work in his office since the work I was doing involved very confidential files, and they could not go home with me, but I was extremely thankful for the work and the hours I was working, which offered me the flexibility to still take my daughter to school and pick her up.

We would not sink after all!

It was at this time I had some members of my family tell me that I should think about "getting a real job." I had a daughter to support, and this was no time to be sitting at home and hoping for work to come in. I assured them that I was doing exactly what I needed to do to gain clients and build my business, but it did not seem they had that much faith in me and what I was capable of.

I became a member of the local Chamber of Commerce, and from there, I was able to connect with people who were local business owners and who would be able to share my business services with others. I also took the Chamber of Commerce member book and went through and reached out to nearly every member in there and told them of my services. Even if they did not need me then and there, they may know of someone who could use my services, or they may need me down the road.

Either way, I made sure the seed was planted.

The next thing I did was get a vehicle decal with my business name and contact information beautifully done by a local company. The first week I had the decal on, I had calls coming in enquiring about my business, and I was even approached in the local Walmart parking lot while shopping with my daughter by a local mortgage broker who was very interested in my services.

Things were beginning to look up!

I posted ads on Kijiji for my services, and I was surprised to be contacted by a very well-established therapist's office where I used to live. The owner was looking for someone to manage the calls and book appointments for the associates in the office. She was happy I was familiar with the area as well since I had just moved from there.

You reap what you sow!

The hard work was finally beginning to pay off. I had more and more calls and e-mail inquiries coming in, and people were contacting me about word-of-mouth references too. I was so excited.

After some time, my landlord, who had given me work, was looking to take early retirement, and I would not have to work in his office any longer. So, I was now faced with really going solo and trusting in my ability to keep my business and us afloat.

Slowly by slowly, my clients came my way. Some were just looking for piece work, but eventually, some were and still are long-term clients. After five years of working hard at building up my business, I can say I am truly satisfied, and we have been truly blessed.

I now have regular monthly clients who are amazing to work for. I now own my own home on 57 beautifully wooded acres. I have also returned to school part-time and have nearly completed my Holistic Nutritional Therapist designation. I own a small hobby farm with dogs, cats, rabbits, goats, chickens, and ducks, and we are preparing for horses in the spring. And in the world, we live in. Currently, I have been afforded the opportunity to be there in whatever way is needed to help my daughter succeed in school too.

The most important lesson I have learned along the way is that you MUST believe in yourself, even when no one else does. You MUST know what your why is so that when those hard days come, and they will, you can keep pushing past the hard stuff. There is no real failure; all the moments that seem hard are there to teach you something.

I say to you, "girl (or guy), *stop making excuses!*". If you really want something in life, GO FOR IT.

There is an amazing reward and blessing waiting at the end of it all if you just keep pushing forward toward your dreams. The *best* part of it all? Telling those who did not believe in you – that YOU DID IT!

Heather Andrews

Speaker, publisher, and best-selling author, Heather Andrews is the founder and CEO of *Get You Visible,* a business empowering entrepreneurs to create their stories and impart their wisdom to the world. As a literary coach, Heather is passionate about how storytelling will uplevel your business, expand your influence, and establish your unique brand. She helps her clients create more impact by sharing their vulnerability and authentic experiences. Let Heather Andrews help you use the power of your story to get visible and get more business!

Connect with Heather:

www.getyouvisible.com

www.facebook.com/getyouvisible

https://www.linkedin.com/in/andrewsheather/

Chapter 12

Road to Reclamation

By Heather Andrews

I remember my days as a healthcare manager when my employees would come to work in a good mood, bad mood, or just distant. As a manager, I knew my employees well enough to know when something was off in their life when they did come to bring their best selves to work. I would ask if there was anything they needed to discuss. It provided an outlet for them if they needed it. Some took it, and others did not, which was fine, but they knew I cared and was there for them. When I was restructured from this job, my heart broke, and I lost my identity. I figured I would consult in my profession, work per diem for applications or work casually at the hospital, as jobs were abundant. I knew I was not working full-time for any company ever again. I was diversifying my skill set and income streams as a result.

It was time for Plan B. This was back in 2015, and if you had told me all of the twists and turns, gains, wins, and losses, including a pandemic, that would take us to 2022. I may not have believed you.

I have discovered entrepreneurs are a special breed, and it is not for the faint of heart. Statistics show that most businesses fail in the first five years. There are many factors: financial, not enough clients, or you grow too fast, and the foundation is not set, the list goes on. I am in my seven years. I am still here, but I have poured 400,000.00 into my company with websites, marketing, staff, investment in coaches, and professional development so I could learn from others. It has been a road worth being on as I have gained so much but lost just as much. I know I would not change a thing because I am free to be me; I am serving others and helping them grow into who they want to be so they can serve.

This journey has taught me so much that no amount of education in a facility ever could. I have spent 33 years in healthcare frontline service to management, consulting, project and change management with international travel. As a mother to three amazing adults, I have learned how to love genuinely. As a wife to an ex-wife, I have learned reclamation of my life and putting myself first to refill my soul. As a daughter, I have loved and cared for my parents and knew that I couldn't live under their expectations forever despite how much; at 51, I want to please and do right by them. I am an individual who finally has claimed my spot and embraced my purpose, which is encompassed in this chapter.

Our stories will change every day, depending on life circumstances and choices. But I know to date, everything I do is from a space of service, love, and passion for wanting the best in humanity, especially living in our times.

I chose my career in healthcare because I wanted to help others, travel, make a good income, and have options to progress in my career. I was accepted into the Medical X-ray technologist program at 18 and graduated at 20. The world was my oyster. I worked full time right away and was rolling in the dough with enjoying life until the recession hit Alberta with massive healthcare cuts, which drove me out of a job. I took control of the situation with the decision in hand to go to live in Saudi Arabia to work in my chosen field. I arrived in July 1994 in Riyadh with a temperature of 45 degrees Celsius on the gauge. Super hot it was. I dawned my black abaya and was driven by our Saudi Driver to our hospital Villas. The next day, I reported for our orientation, where I met people from all over the globe that had come to work at my hospital. The years in Saudi were very rewarding as I stood on my own two feet. I moved to a culture where I did not know anyone and had to embrace their way of life, but I was super-empowered because I lived on my terms. I traveled to Egypt, Jordan, Dubai, Nepal, and Europe. There is nothing like travel to teach you life lessons and make you stand on your own two feet.

While I lived there, I saw the entrepreneurial spirit of foreigners. Alongside working full time, they would clean houses, wash cars, cook for people that did not like to, and cut hair; if they had a skill, they utilized it to make extra money to send home to their loved ones. It was amazing to observe their ambition. This taught me a few lessons as I always wanted my own business or additional revenue stream. While I lived in Saudi, I met the man who I would spend the next 26 years with, raising our family while he served the United States Military with tours to Afghanistan. Little did I know that my job restructuring in 2015 would be the beginning of the end for us.

After my healthcare management restructuring, I enrolled in a coaching program that I loved.

I started networking with other women, which I found empowering. I loved that they took all their knowledge, experience, and corporate backgrounds to start a business they were passionate about. I was invited to attend a Womanition luncheon. I was greeted by the owner Dorothy Briggs. I met a connection that day that changed my life. I was invited to participate in a multi-authored book that would launch on Amazon. This idea intrigued me as I would become a published author. I did not think I could write, but I discovered I could. I enjoyed it. Who Knew? I was invited into a publishing mentorship program to help people self-publish their books. This intrigued me as I always loved hearing people's stories of resiliency.

I had to publish a book of my own to learn the process correctly. I embarked upon bringing 23 people together so they could share their short stories to help inspire others. This took about four months to complete. On our launch day, Obstacles Equal Opportunities hit bestseller. It was the start of something very extraordinary. My publishing company was born. I started sharing my story about how I shifted from a job loss to a business gain. I started speaking in my province about the power of the story. I had pivoted my whole business since I shared mine. I was featured in Alberta's Women's Business Magazine called Womanition. I was invited to speak at their conference. This was the start of the public speaking component of my business. This is where our business started to propel.

I had my team of 1 editor, a graphic book cover designer, and myself. I realized very quickly that I needed more people as authors started coming to me to publish their books. By 2019, I had traveled to many places in the United States to speak on many stages with the likes of Dr. John D. Martini. We had grown to have a waitlist before we could take on more people. In 1 month, we grew from a team of 6 to 27 that included a business manager, podcast manager, editors, proofreaders, and graphic design. The referrals were rolling in; life was good. We served our authors and watching my clients shine made my heart sing.

The business was doing well; we were on our way. Our revenue was off the charts, but so were my expenses.

Growing a team was expensive. I increased my prices, and I took less of a salary, despite we were making six digits. We published over 300 co-authors and authors, 250 podcast interviews, and a 90% rate of best-selling authors.

August of 2019 is etched in my memory forever as life-changing! My marriage fell apart, which had been happening for a while, but neither of us wanted to admit it, so we buried our heads in the sand till one day, the words "I don't want this anymore rolled out of my mouth." Telling our children, who were young adults, was heart-wrenching. I stayed living in our matrimonial home even though we agreed to separate. Two weeks later, I was driving to work, and my phone rang in my car. My mom told me she needed to go to Emergency as she had a massive headache and could not see. She went from fully independent to not in 24 hours. I immediately packed up my clothes and went to stay with her. It was one year of testing and eye surgery for her to get back to somewhat of a normal vision with independence. I was grateful I had my team to keep my business and projects moving forward.

The world changed as we knew in March 2020; the world paused, and so did my business. We canceled my major event, which filled our year of clients commonly. The world leaders said, in 2 weeks, we would be back to normal. Well, as a healthcare professional, I knew this was not the case. As a business owner, I knew I was in trouble. We received a grant that the Canadian Government issued. That kept us alive for three months to pay salaries. I had to reduce my overhead. Hospitals were short, and positions were bountiful, so I went back to frontline healthcare. I stopped pulling a salary from my company altogether. People had halted projects that meant decreased revenue, and some weren't moving forward until there was more certainty in the world. In September of 2020, my contractors found other work, my business manager resigned, and I canceled many platforms we were using to save costs. I borrowed money and paid off my debts. By December 2020, I started coaching to guide people to write their books. I was losing my passion for my business despite loving coaching people to share their stories. I was burnt out. Divorce, separation of my furbaby, helping my mom, working in healthcare, running my company, and trying to keep it going were more than enough. I am a survivor! I will do whatever it takes. I remortgaged, which got me the money I needed to make things simpler. In March of 2021, an opportunity arose that I knew would be life-changing. Womanition South needed a new license holder. It was where my journey began six years ago. I have spoken on their stages and been featured in their magazine over the last four years, which has helped me become an expert in my field as a publisher, story coach, speaker, and author. I made the call on that day in March to Dorothy Briggs to ask if I could discuss how to help her manage the South part of the province. As the months went on, I decided to purchase the license for Womanition South. Dorothy agreed! I have held two significant events to date with speakers and vendors to bring people together again after two long years of covid. People crave connection, and the great resignation happens as they realize they want something different. Entrepreneurs are abounding! The way people do business has changed. Income streams have changed.

Opportunities are abundant despite the obstacles that be presented.

I have given you the fast-paced, cliff note version of my journey. The bottom line is I have come full circle. The road of the entrepreneur is to be willing to pivot, look for the signs when things need to change, and be real about your numbers and bottom line. If you aren't profitable, it is time to turn things in a different direction.

The road traveled has prepared me for where I am propelled to go. I was made to help business owners connect, support, and grow. Helping them embrace their own story makes them unique and trustworthy, creating credibility for their referral partners and clients to increase their income. My lessons have changed my own money story as I am worthy and deserving of my 1,000,000.00 company. The inner circle you chose to travel with you is priceless, with the right advice, guidance, and support.

The five pillars of my publishing company are:

- Courage
- Choice
- Connection
- Creation
- Community

After writing my first chapter in a compiled book, I realized it was these values that I had applied to my journey. These act as my filter for personal and professional decisions I make. Here is how:

Courage:

- Am I honest with myself?

- What story am I telling myself? Will it hold me back or propel me forward?
- Is the course I am on in my life and business working with me to provide:
- Service to my clients, Revenue to my business, Profitability for my future.
- What red flags do I see and feel?
- What makes me happy?
- Reality check: How am I showing up in myself, my clients, my relationships, and the world?
- Am I ready for more, or do I need to pause and do the reality check-in?

Choice:

You have a choice as to how you think and feel. You can choose to encompass fear which will hold you back, or face fear which means "Face everything and Rule." I was more scared to stay where I was than to move forward in my life and onto a new business opportunity.

When making different choices, I do it with facts and approach with curiosity.

I ask myself:

- What could happen if I did this?
- I wonder about this situation.
- Feel the feels around the choice. Your feelings are information.

Connection:

During the dark times in my company, I could have shut it down. I decided not to, as my intuition told me there was a reason to fight for its survival. My 'why' had to be pretty strong.

My story was to inspire others to know that they weren't alone on their journey. Connection is my power. I connect people to their unique stories. From this, I help create a community of aligned and supportive individuals to help them grow their influence.

I ask myself:

- Am I happy with my current situation?
- Am I serving my clients the best way I can?
- Is my company serving me, and my clients and creating a change in the world while making revenue?
- How is my company connecting my community to help others prosper?
- Who am I surrounding myself with so we can make the world better?

Creation:

Being open to different choices and connections can lead to opportunities. New opportunities create new chapters, revenue streams, referral partners, and relationships. Mentorship can lead you to live out your passions and increase your income.

I ask myself when introduced to new opportunities:

- What are the pros and cons?
- How will it grow my network?
- Is it in alignment with what I am doing in this world?
- Will it be profitable as cash is king?

Community:

Through sharing your story, you create a community that bonds and thrives through vulnerability generating influence, impact, and income. Your network becomes your net worth. Through community comes trust and referrals, sharing your story, and inspiring others to do the same.

I ask myself:

- How am I serving myself?
- Am I the change I want to be in my community, business, and the world?
- Is my business risk-proof to sustain world changes?
- Do I have an emergency fund to pay my expenses if the world had an emergency again?

Many lessons have been learned as the only way to overcome an obstacle is to go through it and look for the solution.

Entrepreneurship is a journey. The road will never be boring. The Golden Nugget is to learn from the ones who have gone before you; your mentors are there for you to listen to so you can mitigate a few of the obstacles. Remember, the opportunity is in the obstacle. If things go sideways, remember that there is a road to reclamation when you know you are, have the people to support you, are willing to give it your all, and have the contingency plan and wisdom to know you can achieve success.

Conclusion

Now it's your turn!

As we wrap up this journey through Obstacles Equal Opportunities: Volume III, we hope you're already chomping at the bit to get busy. It's time for you to take control of your situation and overcome your obstacles. The only way past is through.

It's time to put all these strategies, tactics, and tools to work for you as you plot your course around whatever lies in front of you. It's time to reach way down inside of yourself, find your brand of bravery, and jump right in.

It's time to understand that every obstacle you encounter on your path is a blessing in disguise. Knowing that by taking on those challenges with authenticity, vulnerability, and positivity, each is polishing your resiliency until you shine like the diamond I know you are.

And finally, it's time to shimmy. Are you ready?

Love,

Heather

Do You Dream of Being a Published Author?

The best part of what I do is bring people together to write, share, and inspire those who may feel alone or need healing. Your story could help to heal others.

My team will guide you through the writing process, so your idea can become a reality to be shared on worldwide distribution channels.

A book has been referenced as an authority piece for centuries and is known to be one of the best ways to gain instant credibility and visibility with clients in the online and offline space.

Let's talk if you have a story to share and want to become a published author or co-author in a collaborative.

Book your complimentary call with me.

https://followitthru.as.me/tellyourstory

Here's to your story and someone waiting to read it.

Heather

https://getyouvisible.com/

Manufactured by Amazon.ca
Bolton, ON

26177102R00102